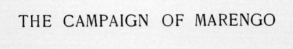

THE CAMPAIGN OF MARENGO

THE
CAMPAIGN OF MARENGO

𝕎ith ℭomments

BY

HERBERT H. SARGENT

FIRST LIEUTENANT AND QUARTERMASTER, SECOND CAVALRY, UNITED
STATES ARMY ; MEMBER OF THE MILITARY HISTORICAL
SOCIETY OF MASSACHUSETTS ;
AUTHOR OF "NAPOLEON BONAPARTE'S FIRST CAMPAIGN"

CHICAGO
A. C. McCLURG AND COMPANY
1897

DEDICATION

BY A SOLDIER

TO

THE SOLDIERS OF HIS COUNTRY

IT is written in a certain book, with which most of us are familiar, that a day will come when there shall be no more wars. But that time is far distant. When the laws of human society change, wars may cease, but not till then. All around us is strife ; the weak are ever falling before the strong. The grass takes its strength from the soil and air, and each blade struggles for food and light with its neighbor. The beast consumes the grass, and man destroys the beast. We struggle on, contending with one another and with the world, and encountering defeat and death when we meet a stronger power than ourselves. Such is Nature's stern law. It regulates the life of the worm that crawls at our feet, governs the actions of men, and determines the destinies of peoples. The conclusion is therefore reached that until man can rise above this law, the time will not come when there shall be no further need of armies, and when war shall be no more.

No country has ever become great without soldiers. They lay the foundations of nations. In
the history of every great people there is a record
of battles fought and battles won. At Lexington,
at Bunker Hill, at Gettysburg, men died that a
nation might live. Is it any wonder that we should
be proud of our profession? "Whoever has a
heart," says Von der Goltz, "feels it beat higher
and becomes enthusiastic for the profession of the
soldier." Napier says: "War is the condition of
this world. From man to the smallest insect, all
are at strife; and the glory of arms, which cannot
be obtained without the exercise of honor, forti-
tude, courage, obedience, modesty, and temper-
ance, excites the brave man's patriotism, and is a
chastening corrective for the rich man's pride."

We cannot know whether we shall be called
upon to fight for our country ; we may be called,
or not; but we shall deserve no less the gratitude
of our countrymen, if we remain *always ready*.
Wars have been necessary in the past; they will
be necessary in the future.

> "Man needs must fight
>   To make true peace his own :
> He needs must combat might with might,
>   Or might would rule alone."

" *The decisive events of the world take place in the intellect.* It is the mission of books that they help one to remember it."

PREFACE

I HAVE written this book for the civilian and the soldier. I cherish the hope that it will be interesting to both.

H. H. S.

FORT WINGATE, NEW MEXICO,
December 7, 1896.

CONTENTS

LIST OF MAPS

AT END OF VOLUME.

THE
CAMPAIGN OF MARENGO.

———◆———

CHAPTER I.

INTRODUCTION.[1]

After a war one ought not only to write the history of what has taken place, but also the history of what was intended. — VON DER GOLTZ.

UPON Bonaparte's return from Egypt in October, 1799, he found England, Austria, and the small states dependent upon them waging war against France. The allies were united in an effort to crush the French Republic. They were sanguine of success. Against this formidable coalition France stood alone.

Before Bonaparte's return, a Russian army, commanded by Suwaroff, had also been fighting the French in Italy and Switzerland; but, having been defeated by Masséna, Suwaroff had retreated with the remnants of his army into the valley of the Danube, and thence had proceeded into Russia. The defeat of Suwaroff had caused the Russian Emperor, Paul the First, to believe that his army had not been properly supported by the Austrian armies. He therefore felt angry and bitter

[1] See Map I.

towards Austria. As soon as Bonaparte became aware of the state of the Emperor's mind he collected the Russian prisoners then in France, gave them new uniforms and new arms, and sent them back to their own country. These acts and others of a conciliatory nature pleased and flattered the Emperor Paul, and enabled Bonaparte, soon after his return, to detach Russia from the alliance.

Of the two great powers at war with France, England had been more active and more successful upon the sea; Austria, upon the land. In the battle of the Nile, Nelson had dealt the French navy a terrible blow, from the effects of which it never recovered. England was now mistress of the sea. Having her fleets in the Mediterranean and the Gulf of Genoa, she was prepared to assist Austria in her efforts to overthrow the French Republic.

During Bonaparte's absence in Egypt, Austria, aided by Russia, had pushed forward her armies to the boundaries of France. One large Austrian army[1] in western Germany was watching the crossings of the Rhine; another in northwestern Italy was fighting the French along the Apennines and Maritime Alps. From the theatre of operations made memorable by Bonaparte's victories

---

[1] Though troops from several of the small German States dependent upon Austria formed a part of this army, it is referred to as an "Austrian army," because the bulk of the troops composing it were Austrians.

in 1796–97, Austria had almost driven the French eagles. Bonaparte's battles of Montenotte, Lodi, Castiglione, Arcole, and Rivoli seemed to have been won in vain. Austria had all but reconquered Italy. Except along the narrow seaboard between the Apennines and the sea, no French soldiers were to be found upon Italian soil.

Such was the situation when, in November, 1799, Bonaparte became First Consul of France. At this time his acts certainly indicated a desire for peace. He wrote to the governments of England and Austria, deploring the futility of a continuation of the conflict, and suggesting that the war should cease. His overtures, however, were coldly rejected. He was forced to fight. Against this powerful coalition peace could be obtained only by victorious battle.

Industriously Bonaparte prepared for war. France was in a deplorable state. The treasury was empty ; the soldiers were ill fed and ill clad ; recruits and supplies were obtained with difficulty ; civil war existed in certain parts of western France ; and the armies of the Republic had met with defeat again and again. Over the French people this condition of affairs had cast a gloom which the magic of Bonaparte's name alone could dispel.

During the winter of 1799–1800 his energy and activity were apparent everywhere. His proclamations aroused the spirit and patriotism of the

French people, and gave them confidence in their government, and hope of success under his leadership. He placed the finances upon a firm basis, crushed out the civil war, caused arms to be manufactured, and supplies to be collected ; and from the levies that he ordered he organized sufficient forces to strengthen materially the French military power. Of the two French armies in the field, he sent re-enforcements to the Army of the Rhine, gave the command of it to General Moreau, and ordered General Masséna to take command of the Army of Italy, which, half-starved upon the rocks of Genoa, was struggling heroically against overwhelming odds. At this time, too, he began to collect, drill, and organize, in different parts of France, bodies of men who were destined to unite near Lake Geneva, and together with other troops in France already organized, were to form a third army, to be known as the Army of Reserve.

Before entering into the details of the campaign, it is necessary to describe the topography of the theatre of operations, to point out the situations of the opposing forces, and to explain the plans of the contending powers.

Bordering France on the east are Germany, Switzerland, and Italy. The Alps, covering Switzerland like a huge network, give to this country the appearance of an immense bastion, which, extending east, separates Germany from Italy. From Switzerland these mountains extend through

and beyond the Tyrol. They separate the valley of
the Danube from the valley of the Po. In Switzerland they are known as the Swiss Alps; in the
Tyrol, as the Tyrolese Alps. On the north side
of them are the States of Swabia, Bavaria, and
Upper Austria; on the south side, Piedmont,
Lombardy, and Venice.

Extending south from western Switzerland to
within about thirty miles of the sea, the French
Alps form part of the boundary line between
France and Italy; thence, turning east, they approach the Italian shore, and are here known as
the Maritime Alps; still farther east, along the
shores of the Gulf of Genoa, they are called the
Apennines.

With the exception of a few passes, this great
mountain chain, almost enclosing northern Italy,
forms an insurmountable barrier to the soldier.
Even over the passes, especially across the higher
ranges, communication was, at the time of which
we write, extremely dangerous. The snow and ice,
the glaciers, avalanches, frequent storms, and steep
declivities, made these mountain roads hazardous
and difficult for the passage of armies. The principal passes in the Swiss Alps are the St. Gothard,
the Simplon, and the Great St. Bernard; in the
French Alps, the Little St. Bernard, and the Mont
Cenis; in the Maritime Alps, the Col di Tenda
and the Col di Ormea; and in the Apennines, the
Col di Cadibona and the Bochetta.

Lying partly or entirely within this territory are three large rivers and their tributaries. They have their sources in or near the great chain of the Alps, and drain the tributary country. The Po rises in the French Alps, and flows east through northern Italy. The Danube rises in western Germany, and flows east through Bavaria and Austria. The Rhine rises in Switzerland, flows north into Lake Constance, thence, forming the outlet of the lake, flows west to Bâle, where it turns abruptly and flows north for the rest of its course.

Early in April, 1800, an Austrian army of one hundred and twenty thousand soldiers, commanded by Marshal Kray, guarded the right bank of the upper Rhine. The right wing extended beyond Strasburg; the left, well up into the Alps east of Switzerland; and the centre, forming the greater part of Kray's army, occupied the Black Forest in the angle of the Rhine made by its change of direction at Bâle. Kray's line of communication was along several roads down the Danube to the Austrian capital.

Facing the Austrian army, on the opposite side of the river, was the Army of the Rhine, commanded by Moreau. Including the French forces in Switzerland, it numbered one hundred and thirty thousand soldiers, and extended from the St. Gothard on the right to Strasburg on the left. It had for a base of operations the frontier fortresses of France, and Switzerland, which was occupied by the French.

The Austrian army in northwestern Italy consisted of one hundred and twenty thousand soldiers, and was commanded by General Melas. The greater part of it was in the vicinity of Genoa and along the Apennines and Maritime Alps. The remainder, occupying the fortresses and guarding the entrances to the passes of the Alps, was scattered throughout northwestern Italy. This army had its base of operations on the Mincio; and its line of communication was by several roads down the valley of the Po to its base, thence by two roads: one north through the Tyrol across the Brenner Pass into the valley of the Danube; the other northeast through Friuli across the Pontebba Pass to Vienna.

Opposed to the army of Melas was the Army of Italy. It consisted of forty thousand soldiers, of whom thirty-six thousand, commanded by Masséna, were holding the passes of the Apennines and Maritime Alps from Genoa to the Col di Tenda. The remainder, four thousand strong, commanded by General Thurreau, was guarding the Mont Cenis Pass in the French Alps. The line of communication of the Army of Italy to its base of operations on the Rhone was by the Genoa-Nice road.

A British fleet, commanded by Admiral Keith was in the Gulf of Genoa; and a British corps twelve thousand strong, commanded by General Abercromby, was at Port Mahon in Minorca.

Such were the main features of the theatre of operations, and such were the positions and numbers of the opposing armies that were facing each other in Germany, France, Switzerland, and Italy, at the beginning of hostilities early in April, 1800. Against the Austrian armies, supported by the British navy, and a British corps which might at any time be thrown upon the coast of France, Bonaparte could not, with his two armies, expect to make much headway. His chances of success were small; the odds against him were too great. Unless he could increase his own forces, a French victory was doubtful. Thus it was that early in the winter he had seen the necessity of creating an army of reserve, which could be sent to re-enforce Moreau in Germany or Masséna in Italy as circumstances might require. But the Army of Reserve had not yet been assembled. The divisions composing it were still scattered throughout France. Their organization, however, was being rapidly pushed forward, with the intention that early in May they should unite near Lake Geneva and form an army of forty thousand soldiers.

On the French side, Bonaparte, at the head of the French Republic, had for the first time full control of all military operations. Hitherto, great as had been his achievements in Italy and in Egypt, he had acted as a subordinate, merely directing the operations of his own army; but now his military genius was to have full play.

On the Austrian side, the Aulic Council, consisting of twenty-one members, directed all military operations. This council, which held its sessions at Vienna, not only made the plans of campaign, but also issued detailed orders to the Austrian commanders, and furnished them information regarding Bonaparte's plans and manœuvres.

At this time the ablest soldier in Austria was the Archduke Charles. Already he had greatly distinguished himself in several campaigns. He reasoned that, inasmuch as Austria, England, and Russia had failed to crush the French Republic in 1799, before Bonaparte's return to France, the allies stood little hope of success after Russia had withdrawn from one side, and Bonaparte had been added to the other. He therefore advised his government to accept Bonaparte's offer of peace. To the Aulic Council he also gave valuable advice upon the military situation. But no attention was paid to his suggestions. In fact, before the campaign opened, the Archduke was relieved of his command in the army, and sent into Bohemia in a kind of honorable exile.

The plan of campaign adopted by the allies was that the Austrian army under Kray in Germany should remain on the defensive, holding Moreau in check if possible, while the Austrian army under Melas in Italy attacked the Army of Italy along the Apennines and Maritime Alps. By this means, the allies expected that the Austrian forces in Italy, so superior in numbers to the French, would be able with the help of the British fleet to blockade Genoa, and to drive the Army of Italy across the Var into southern France. This movement being accomplished, the purpose was that Melas, supported by the British navy and Abercromby's corps, should invade France, and attack and capture Toulon. Furthermore, the allies hoped, by adopting this plan, to receive some support from the Royalists in the south of France. If this operation succeeded, it was expected that Moreau would detach a sufficient force from the Army of the Rhine to march on Toulon for the purpose of driving back the allies: whereupon Kray could attack the Army of the Rhine, thus weakened, with much hope of success; that, in fact, he could take the offensive, force the crossings of the Rhine, and invade France.

In this calculation no plans were made to attack the French forces in the great stronghold of Switzerland. If, however, the allies succeeded in their designs, Kray and Melas could unite their armies in France, thus cut the communications of the French forces in Switzerland, and smother them, as it were, between the two great Austrian armies.

In view of the facts that the allies were flushed

with their recent victories, were superior to their adversary in numbers, and also held the mastery of the sea, they expected great results in the coming campaign. With so many advantages on their side, their plans seemed both reasonable and accomplishable; but they reckoned without the genius of Bonaparte.

On the other side, Bonaparte had two plans, both of which it will be well to examine, that the reader may grasp the breadth of Bonaparte's intellect in originating strategic conceptions. Both plans were based upon the fact that the great stronghold of Switzerland, extending like a huge wedge between the Austrian army in Germany and that in Italy, was occupied by the French. This natural fortress, almost impregnable, could be used as a base of operations from which to attack either Kray in Germany or Melas in Italy.

The first plan conceived by Bonaparte was to leave Masséna in Italy on the defensive to hold Melas in check, then to unite the Army of Reserve with Moreau's army, cross the Rhine in force between Schaffhausen and Lake Constance, and attack that part of Kray's army occupying the Black Forest in the angle of the Rhine between Lake Constance and Strasburg. By an attack in this direction, Bonaparte calculated that he could defeat Kray, drive him north, sever his communications with Vienna, and either destroy or capture his army. If successful in this operation, he could descend the Danube and seize the Emperor's capital; then by taking possession of the Tyrol and the Carnic Alps, he could occupy the Brenner and Pontebba passes, which operation would sever the communications of Melas in Italy and cut him off from Vienna. With Kray's army captured or destroyed, with the French holding the only passes by which the Austrians in Italy could retreat, and with Bonaparte in possession of the Austrian capital, the campaign must end; the Austrian Emperor would be compelled to make peace. This plan had many advantages. It would, if successful, be far-reaching in its results; it would not only destroy Kray, but would paralyze the operations of Melas; it would, to use Bonaparte's expressive words, "reconquer Italy at Vienna."

Though this plan promised great results it was not carried out. A rivalry between Moreau and Bonaparte was the principal cause. The former, being jealous of the latter, refused to serve under him. Though the First Consul had shown his confidence in Moreau, and, by appointing him to command the Army of the Rhine, had recognized his great military abilities, nevertheless Moreau objected to having Bonaparte direct the operations of the combined armies in person. In fact, he stated that he would send in his resignation if the First Consul took command of the Army of the Rhine. At a later day this would undoubtedly have resulted in Moreau's losing his command;

but at this time Bonaparte was not in a position to force a quarrel with him. He had need of Moreau's great military talents. Furthermore, the commander of the Army of the Rhine had the unbounded confidence of the soldiers under him, and was at that time the only general in France, except Masséna and Bonaparte himself, who was able to direct successfully the operations of a large army. Victory was Bonaparte's object. To be victorious, it was necessary to utilize the services of every great soldier of France.

Doubtless, too, in adopting another plan, Bonaparte was influenced somewhat by the hope of gaining a great victory with the army that he himself had created. If he could cross the Alps with the Army of Reserve and strike a blow which would decide the fate of Italy, he alone would reap the glory. Moreover, by following in the footsteps of Hannibal, he would be more likely to dazzle the French people, and to fix deeply in their minds the splendor of his achievements.

Bonaparte's second plan was that Moreau should cross the Rhine and attack Kray in such a direction as to push him back from Lake Constance towards the north; that he should then detach a corps of twenty or twenty-five thousand soldiers from his army and send them across Switzerland by the St. Gothard Pass into Italy, where they were to unite with the Army of Reserve to be led by Bonaparte in person over the Great St. Bernard Pass. With these forces Bonaparte purposed to march south, cross the Po, seize the line of retreat of the Austrians, and force them to fight a battle to recover their communications.

Should he succeed in this manœuvre, a single victorious battle would decide the fate of the Austrians in Italy; for it would sever their communications and cut them from their base of operations. To Melas, therefore, a defeat would mean the ruin, capture, or annihilation of his army; to Austria it would mean the loss of Italy.

The success of this plan depended upon the skill with which Bonaparte could deceive the Austrians in Italy as to his intentions; for should they learn of the existence of the Army of Reserve, and of Bonaparte's intention to cross the Great St. Bernard, they could concentrate near the Italian entrance to the pass, and overwhelm the French divisions in detail as they issued into Italy. It was necessary, therefore, that the strength, destination, even the existence of the Army of Reserve, should be kept as secret as possible. To accomplish this, Bonaparte published in the newspapers, and announced in various ways, that the Army of Reserve was assembling at Dijon in France, and that it would soon be sent to re-enforce the Army of Italy. At the same time he took care to collect there only a few thousand men, consisting mostly of conscripts and old soldiers.

The wide publicity given the matter caused the

spies of England and Austria to gather at Dijon, but finding there only unorganized conscripts and veterans too old for active service, they sent word to their governments that no such army existed. Consequently the Army of Reserve was believed to be imaginary, and was ridiculed and caricatured throughout Europe.

Both Melas and Kray were completely deceived. Feeling certain that there were but two French armies with which to contend, they had great hope of success. Moreover, the information received from the Aulic Council confirmed them in this opinion. Melas, in particular, regarded the matter as a ruse of Bonaparte, intended to divert the Austrians in Italy from invading France. He therefore felt secure in his positions, and pushed forward his forces with renewed energy. Feeling certain that he had fathomed Bonaparte's stratagem, he rested in a security which doomed him to defeat.

Meanwhile the divisions of the Army of Reserve were concentrating. They were marching through France; and were rapidly assembling near Geneva, from which place they were to be led across the Alps into Italy. This army, so secretly organized, and so derided throughout Europe; this army, whose very existence was doubted by the allies, was destined to amaze the world by the brilliancy of its exploits. Bonaparte will lead it over the Great St. Bernard Pass across the Alps, descend like an avalanche into the valley of the Po, cut the communications of the Austrians, and defeat them in the hard-fought battle of Marengo. He will emulate the deeds of Hannibal. He will lead forty thousand soldiers across the highest mountains of Europe, surmount every obstacle in his pathway, overthrow every force sent to oppose his progress, and by a single march and a single battle reconquer northern Italy.

COMMENTS.

In making war upon France the Austrian forces were obliged to advance along both the Danube and the Po; for if they confined their operations exclusively to the valley of the Danube, they must yield northern Italy to the French; or if they restricted their operations wholly to the valley of the Po, they must lose western Germany, and leave unguarded the direct route between France and Austria. The Austrian forces were, therefore, divided into two armies: one of which confined its operations to the valley of the Danube; the other, to the valley of the Po. In advancing towards France, these armies became farther and farther separated from each other. Kray's army in western Germany and the army of Melas in northwestern Italy were separated by Switzerland and the great chain of the Alps. As Switzerland and the passes of the Swiss Alps were held by the

French, there could be no direct communication between Kray and Melas. Though the great highway of the Tyrol, which crossed the Alps over the Brenner Pass, was in possession of the Austrians, it was so far in rear of the Austrian armies that re-enforcements could not be sent over it from one army to the other without making a march of several hundred miles. In fact, the nature of the country was such that during active operations neither army could expect to receive any support from the other. They were independent armies of equal strength. Each had a separate commander, and each had its own line of operations and its own line of retreat.

On the other hand, the three French armies were so situated that they could support one another. With Moreau's army on the Rhine, Masséna's along the Apennines, and the Army of Reserve between them near Lake Geneva, Bonaparte could move the last along the roads of eastern France to re-enforce either of the others as circumstances might require. In this way Bonaparte could re-enforce Masséna with the Army of Reserve, which would increase the Army of Italy to eighty thousand combatants. Or, should Masséna be driven back across the Var into France, Bonaparte could leave Moreau on the defensive along the Rhine with a part of his army, withdraw the remainder, unite it with the Army of Reserve, and with these combined forces added to the remnants of Masséna's army, destroy Melas in the south of France.

Had the Austrian armies succeeded in invading France simultaneously, Bonaparte would have detached a containing force [1] against one army, and then have massed his remaining forces against the other. By repeating this manœuvre, first against one army and then against the other, he would have attempted to defeat both. In this case, the Austrian armies would enter France from different directions; one from the east, the other from the southeast, separated by Switzerland and the French Alps; and since the French armies, even while falling back, would still be between the Austrian armies, Bonaparte would, from his central position, have the advantage of interior lines, and could rapidly combine his forces against his adversaries in succession.

How well he would have succeeded in this manœuvre can best be judged by what he accomplished by similar manœuvres.

In the Italian campaign of 1796–97, when the Austrians advanced against Bonaparte on both sides of Lake Garda, he united his forces at the foot of the lake; and, by throwing a strong force against one and then against the other of the

---

[1] Containing force. A body of troops charged with the duty of holding in check a body (generally numerically superior) of the enemy, while the main efforts of the army are directed against another portion of the hostile forces. — WAGNER.

advancing armies, defeated both in succession before they could unite. In these manœuvres, with a total force of forty-five thousand soldiers, he defeated seventy-two thousand Austrians.

In the campaigns of Arcole and Rivoli, the Austrians likewise advanced with divided forces. In the former, forty thousand Frenchmen opposed seventy thousand Austrians; in the latter, forty-four thousand Frenchmen opposed sixty-five thousand Austrians. By skilful combinations, similar to those just described, Bonaparte defeated the Austrian armies in both campaigns.

In 1814, when the Prussians, under Blucher, and the Austrians, under Schwarzenberg, were advancing from different points of the French frontier upon Paris, the results obtained by Napoleon's leaving a retarding force before one army, and by massing his remaining forces against the other, were still more remarkable. With a force numerically inferior to either army opposed to him, he succeeded in winning battle after battle. Though in the campaign of 1814 we find strategical problems with which we are not now concerned, yet Napoleon's victories there in the face of such odds show what he might have accomplished had Kray and Melas crossed the French frontiers and advanced on Paris.

But the combination that offered Bonaparte the greatest chance of success yet remains to be considered. Should Masséna be able single-handed to hold in check the Austrians in Italy, Bonaparte could unite the Army of Reserve, forty thousand strong, to Moreau's army of one hundred and thirty thousand. This junction would give Bonaparte one hundred and seventy thousand soldiers with whom to attack the one hundred and twenty thousand Austrians under Kray. With such a superiority in numbers, Bonaparte would probably have annihilated the Austrian forces in the valley of the Danube.

But the mere superiority in numbers, which, by this combination, might have been obtained in Germany, is not the only advantage which Bonaparte could have derived from the positions of the opposing armies. In order to understand the subject better and see, perhaps, in a measure, the whole strategical situation as it appeared to Bonaparte himself, it will be necessary to examine somewhat carefully the positions of the opposing forces, and point out the advantages which the possession of Switzerland gave to the French.

Since Moreau's army was in position in France along the west bank of the Rhine from Strasburg to Bâle, and extended into Switzerland along the south bank of the Rhine from Bâle to Lake Constance, Bonaparte could use either France or Switzerland as a base of operations from which to attack the Austrians in the Black Forest. This angular base gave to Bonaparte a great advantage. His adversary could not know on which side to expect him. By making demonstrations on one side, Bonaparte might deceive Kray as to the real point of attack; then, by massing his forces on the other, he might surprise and overwhelm him. Moreover, by crossing the Rhine in force between Lake Constance and Schaffhausen, he could strike the left flank of the Austrian divisions in the Black Forest, and might be able to defeat them in detail before they could unite. Even should Kray succeed in concentrating his divisions, he would be compelled to face south in order to give battle. In this position, his line of battle being parallel to his line of retreat, he must, if defeated, lose his communications. In this position, defeat meant ruin to his army; for with the loss of his communications he could not escape capture or annihilation.

On the other hand, Bonaparte's line of battle would face the north, and be perpendicular to his line of retreat. If defeated, he could fall back and cross the Rhine with little danger of losing his communications.

By uniting the Army of Reserve to Moreau's army, and by crossing the Rhine in force near Schaffhausen, Bonaparte could not only greatly outnumber Kray upon the battle-field, but could force him to fight in a position where an Austrian defeat would be fatal to the Austrian cause. By this manœuvre Bonaparte would threaten the communications of the enemy without exposing his own, and would, if victorious, decide in a single battle the fate of the Austrians in the valley of the Danube. He could then march rapidly upon the Austrian capital, and could seize the Brenner and Pontebba passes, the possession of which would sever the communications of the Austrians in the valley of the Po. Such a manœuvre would paralyze the operations of Melas in Italy, and compel the Austrian Emperor to sue for peace.

Though this plan offered Bonaparte great results, yet in several respects it was somewhat difficult to execute. In order to gain a favorable position for attacking Kray in the Black Forest, Bonaparte would have to make a flank march from Bâle to Lake Constance; and consequently would have to expose his own flank to the attacks of the enemy. But in this case the French flank would be protected by the Rhine; and as Bonaparte would march rapidly, he would in all probability succeed in crossing the river in force near Lake Constance before his adversary should discover his plan. Nevertheless, this flank march would be attended with considerable danger. In fact, every flank march in the vicinity of an active enemy is dangerous; for a commander who gains a position on the enemy's flank must necessarily expose his own flank to the attacks of the enemy. Even when his flank is protected by a river, he cannot cross it without taking some risks. Had Kray's army been assembled in force near Schaffhausen, where it could have attacked the French divisions in detail as they crossed the Rhine, Bonaparte would have had much difficulty in carrying out successfully this plan of campaign. " Of all the operations of war," says Jomini, " there is none more hazardous and difficult than the passage of a large river in the presence of an enemy."

Had Bonaparte adopted this plan, he would undoubtedly have attempted to deceive Kray as to the real point of attack. If we form a judgment of what he would have done by what he afterwards did in the Ulm campaign, we can safely assume that he would have ordered at least one division to cross the Rhine from France, and to advance directly eastward upon Kray's army in the Black Forest. The march of this division would have deceived Kray, and would probably have led him to expect the entire French army from that direction. Bonaparte could then have made his flank march in safety, and could have crossed the river with little danger of having his divisions defeated in detail.

As a matter of fact, however, Kray had his army so widely dispersed that he could not in any case have concentrated a sufficient force in time to oppose successfully the progress of Bonaparte. Even had he been able to assemble his entire army near Schaffhausen, it is doubtful whether, in the face of such odds, he could have prevented Bonaparte from crossing the river. Perhaps it will be well to substantiate this statement by an example. In the two passages of the Danube by Napoleon at Lobau near Vienna in 1809, the difficulties were greater and the odds less than in the hypothetical case now before us. Furthermore, in these operations Napoleon was opposed by that illustrious soldier, the Archduke Charles. Surely, these facts warrant the conclusion that an army of one hundred and seventy thousand soldiers, led by the greatest captain of modern times, could have successfully crossed the Rhine in spite of one hundred and twenty thousand Austrians, commanded by Marshal Kray.

That Bonaparte could have executed this plan of campaign admits of little doubt. We have already shown why the plan was not adopted. But it is worthy of notice that afterwards, in the Ulm campaign, along almost identical lines, he carried out this great strategic conception with remarkable results. It is worthy of notice that, in 1805 at Ulm in the valley of the Danube, he captured an Austrian army, under General Mack, by manœuvres similar to those by which in 1800 he purposed to overwhelm Marshal Kray in the Black Forest. It is worthy of notice that he then descended the Danube, and seized the Austrian capital, and that this march paralyzed to a certain extent the operations of the Archduke Charles in Italy. It is worthy of notice that this march was the principal cause which led the Archduke Charles to retreat before Masséna; and that the Archduke's army would have been captured or destroyed, had not Napoleon been compelled to march north from Vienna in order to meet the Austrian and Russian armies on the field of Austerlitz.

Consider now the situation in northwestern Italy. Since the French were holding the Apennines and Maritime Alps on the south, the French Alps on the west, and Switzerland on the north, they were in possession of the three sides of a rectangle, which almost enclosed Melas in Italy. Should Bonaparte decide to take the offensive there, he could attack the Austrians from the south, from the west, or from the north. This situation gave him several advantages; for Melas could not know on which side to expect the French. Bonaparte might surprise his adversary; he might deceive him as to the real point of attack, and then mass his forces at some unexpected point where he would have the advantage of position.

On the other hand, Melas within the rectangle had the advantage of interior lines. He could therefore, other things being equal, concentrate his forces more quickly upon any side than could Bonaparte. Should he learn in time where Bonaparte would enter Italy, he could defeat the French divisions in detail as they issued from the passes of the Alps. But in order to take advantage of his central position, he must be accurately informed of Bonaparte's movements. He must fathom his

adversary's designs; otherwise the advantage of
position could avail him nothing. Thus it is seen
how the element of surprise became such an essential factor in these operations, and how important
it was that Bonaparte should deceive the Austrians
as to his real intentions. The success of the entire
plan, the fate of Italy itself, hinged on this fact.
It was the first great step towards success; it was
the entering wedge to victory. Long before the
campaign opened, Bonaparte saw clearly this fact.
In the midst of untiring activity at Paris, while
momentous questions were engaging his attention,
he contrived the stratagem that deceived his adversary, and worked out the details that led ultimately
to his triumph at Marengo.

Already some of the advantages which the possession of Switzerland gave to Bonaparte have
been pointed out. It will now be noticed that
he could safely assemble a large force in this
almost impregnable stronghold, and could debouch therefrom upon the rear of the Austrians
in Italy. In this way he could descend upon the
Austrian communications with little danger of
losing his own with Switzerland. Even should the
army of Italy be driven back to the line of the
Var, as long as the French held this river and
the French Alps on one side of the Austrians,
and Switzerland on the other, Bonaparte had the
advantage of an angular base, from either side of
which he could march to attack the Austrians in

Italy. In fact, the possession of Switzerland, extending east from the French frontier, gave to Bonaparte the advantage of an angular base in his operations against either Kray in Germany or Melas in Italy. Moreover, Switzerland offered him a secure place where he could assemble his forces and strike either Austrian army a vital blow. Upon these facts was based not only the plan of campaign that decided the fate of Italy, but that grander conception which offered still greater results.

As previously stated, the Austrian plan of campaign was that Kray should remain on the defensive in Germany, while Melas took the offensive in Italy. There were several reasons for adopting this plan.

First: Austria had in the preceding year been remarkably successful in northern Italy. Step by step she had driven the French from the Adige to the Apennines. Being anxious to hold what she had conquered, and hoping to continue her success in Italy, she gave Melas one hundred and twenty thousand soldiers, and directed him to take the offensive against Masséna.

Second: By making her principal efforts there, she could receive the support of the British fleet in the Gulf of Genoa, and possibly that of the British corps in Minorca.

Third: The English favored this plan; for they saw in it a chance to gain possession of Toulon, which was a desirable acquisition on account of the naval establishments there.

Fourth: The Royalists of southeastern France were in sympathy with England and Austria, and might possibly aid them at the first opportunity.

Fifth: Since Austrià knew that Moreau's army was large, and that the Army of Italy was small, she believed that, by taking the defensive in Germany and the offensive in Italy, she could hold in check the larger army, while she overwhelmed the smaller with greatly superior numbers.

Consider for a moment the situation as it must have appeared at this time to Austria. Not aware of the existence of the Army of Reserve, she saw only Moreau's army along the Rhine, and Masséna's along the Apennines. Was it not reasonable to suppose that the one hundred and twenty thousand Austrians in Germany might hold in check Moreau's army of one hundred and thirty thousand, while the one hundred and twenty thousand Austrians in Italy destroyed the forty thousand French under Masséna?

On the other hand, there were several reasons why this plan should not have been adopted by the Aulic Council.

With the Army of Italy in possession of the Apennines and Maritime Alps, flanked on the right by the fortified city of Genoa, Masséna had the advantage of a strong defensive position. Without an enormous superiority in numbers, it was a difficult matter for Melas to drive back the French. And even should he succeed in this undertaking, there still remained the line of the Var, a strongly fortified position, flanked on the north by the Alps and on the south by the sea; a position which could neither be turned nor be forced, except with greatly superior numbers and desperate fighting.

To succeed offensively in Italy, the Austrians had therefore to outnumber greatly the French. The French superiority in position counterbalanced the Austrian superiority in numbers. The Austrian plan allowed Bonaparte with inferior forces to hold in check for a time a large Austrian army in Italy, and left him free to direct his remaining forces upon the important points of the theatre of operations. By uniting the Army of Reserve with Moreau's army, he could outnumber his adversary in Germany; or by uniting the Army of Reserve with a corps of Moreau's army, he could descend upon the rear of Melas, and decide in a single battle the fate of Italy.

By remaining on the defensive in Germany, Kray gave Bonaparte the opportunity of taking the offensive there. This allowed him to make use of the angular base of operations formed by eastern France and northern Switzerland. Bonaparte, however, could derive no advantage from the angular base except by taking the offensive; for should he simply defend the line of the Rhine, he would be obliged to occupy both the Swiss and French sides of the river. In other words, he would be obliged to divide his forces, to lengthen and weaken his line, thus giving his adversary the opportunity either to defeat the French forces in detail, or to force a passage across the river at some weak point. Furthermore, it was important that Bonaparte should take the offensive for other reasons than those already given; for should he once force the position of the Rhine and Black Forest, he would find no other great natural obstacles in his front as he descended the Danube towards the Austrian capital.

Because the strong position of the Rhine and Black Forest is a long distance from Austria; because the more direct route between France and Austria is through the valley of the Danube; because no great natural obstacles, forming strong defensive positions, lie across this route near the Austrian capital; and because a French victory in the valley of the Danube would probably give the French commander an opportunity to make such dispositions as should paralyze the operations of an Austrian army in Italy, — it follows that the main effort for supremacy between France and Austria should take place in the valley of the Danube. There Austria should take the offensive; there she should show her full strength; there she should make one mighty effort to decide her own or her adversary's fate. " It is in the valley of the Danube," says the Archduke Charles, "that the blows are to be struck which are decisive of the fate of France or Austria."

Austria did exactly the reverse of what she should have done. By taking the offensive in Italy, and by remaining on the defensive in Germany, she gave Bonaparte the opportunity to remain on the defensive in Italy and to take the offensive in Germany. She gave him the opportunity to carry out a plan of campaign which offered him the greatest results, — a plan which was perhaps, on the whole, one of the grandest strategic projects ever conceived by the mind of man.

" To invade a country," says Napoleon, " upon a double line of operations is a faulty combination." Though the Austrian plan was that Kray should remain on the defensive in Germany, while Melas took the offensive in Italy, yet both armies were, under certain circumstances, expected to invade France. Separated as they were by impassable obstacles, Bonaparte could leave a containing force to hold one in check, while he massed overwhelming numbers to crush the other. Thus by adopting a double line of operations, Austria gave Bonaparte the opportunity of bringing superior numbers against either Austrian army. As the first principle of war is to be stronger than the enemy at the vital point, it is always of the greatest importance that no plan of campaign be adopted which shall, at the very start, allow the enemy to

bring superior numbers upon the battle-field.   For
the battle-field *is* the vital point.

The error of adopting a double line of operations
might easily have been avoided by Austria.   Had
she left fifty thousand soldiers in Italy to hold Masséna in check, and concentrated one hundred and
ninety thousand in Germany to act on the offensive,
she would have confined her main efforts to the
more important route between France and Austria,
and would have had greater chances of success.

Had this plan been followed, Bonaparte could
not, by any strategical combination, have outnumbered the Austrians in Germany.   Since it
was necessary that the Army of Italy should
remain along the Apennines and Maritime Alps to
prevent the invasion of France on that side, the
maximum strength which Bonaparte could direct
against the Austrians in Germany was Moreau's
army of one hundred and thirty thousand and the
Army of Reserve, forty thousand strong.   In other
words, Bonaparte could bring only one hundred
and seventy thousand Frenchmen to oppose one
hundred and ninety thousand Austrians.

Furthermore, northern Italy offered Melas many
advantages for a defensive campaign.   If hard
pressed by Masséna, he could fall back to the
Mincio, a strong position, flanked on the right by
Lake Garda and on the left by the fortress of
Mantua.   If defeated in this position, he could
retire into the Tyrol, where he would directly cover

his communications with the valley of the Danube. In the mountains and defiles of the Tyrol, he could, if hard pressed, fall back to another strong position, fight again, and thus prolong the conflict. Moreover, Masséna could not advance eastward through Friuli towards Austria so long as fifty thousand Austrians remained in the Tyrol; for they could then descend upon the flank and rear of the Army of Italy, and could sever the French communications without exposing their own to Masséna's attacks. Of still greater importance, however, is the fact that, had Masséna driven Melas through the Tyrol, or across the Carnic Alps, his success would have had little or no effect upon the operations of the one hundred and ninety thousand Austrians in the valley of the Danube. And why? Because the route between France and Austria through northern Italy was longer than that through the valley of the Danube. Because the mountains of Austria on the side towards Italy offered strong defensive positions near the Austrian capital. Because the vital point of the theatre of operations was in western Germany, and not in northern Italy.

The proof of this will be apparent when we examine the Italian campaign of 1796–97. Though Bonaparte fought his way through northern Italy, and crossed the Alps into Austria, this movement had scarcely any effect upon the operations of the Austrian army that was facing the two French armies, under Moreau and Hoche, on the Rhine in the vicinity of the Black Forest.

In this discussion it has been assumed, in order to point out some of the advantages of a defensive campaign in northern Italy, that forty thousand Frenchmen, commanded by Masséna, might have driven fifty thousand Austrians, under Melas, from the Apennines to and even beyond the Mincio. But this assumption is altogether improbable. Undoubtedly Melas could have held in check the Army of Italy along the Apennines. To prove this statement, consider for a moment what Bonaparte did in the same theatre of operations in 1796. Though he defeated fifty thousand allies with forty thousand Frenchmen, his success was due in great measure to the faulty position of the allies. They were greatly subdivided and separated. Their front was widely extended. At Montenotte he broke through their long line, then defeated them in detail at Millesimo, Dego, and Mondovi. Their faulty position was due to the fact that the Sardinian army, based upon Turin, and the Austrian army, based upon the Mincio, were attempting to cover their divergent lines of communication back to their bases of operations. Moreover, as they fell back along these divergent lines, they became farther and farther separated from each other. The error of separating their armies and of scattering their forces, caused by the attempt to cover directly their communications, made it easier for Bonaparte to defeat them than if they had been united into a single army, and had adopted a single base of operations. For Masséna to defeat fifty thousand Austrians, based upon the Mincio, would therefore be a more difficult undertaking than was that of Bonaparte in 1796. But to do even what Bonaparte did in the early days of the first Italian campaign required a greater soldier than Masséna, — a Frederick himself might have failed.

To the plan of campaign that we have suggested, there was one objection: Marshal Kray did not have sufficient military ability to handle an army of one hundred and ninety thousand soldiers. To direct successfully the operations of so large an army is a great undertaking. Even to command and care for a much smaller one is no small task. Hundreds of matters must be carefully considered. Not only the strategical and tactical manœuvres by which the commander concentrates his forces and wins his victories, but his communications, his means of transportation, the supplies for his army, the equipment and discipline of his troops, the abilities of his subordinate commanders, the topography and resources of the country, give him the greatest anxiety. He must give close attention to all these matters; for the neglect of a single one may lead to disaster. He must be brave, clear-headed, cool, cautious, and fearless; and be able to make a quick decision in critical times. He must have an eye for facts. He must weigh

4

correctly all reports and rumors, and out of the doubtful information at hand sift the true from the false. He must see everything that is going on around him. His glance must penetrate the enemy's line, his vision sweep the whole theatre of operations.

As an army increases in size, so, likewise, the difficulties of commanding it increase. To manœuvre one hundred and ninety thousand soldiers, so as to obtain from them a fighting power proportionate to their numbers, requires the genius of a great captain. Neither Marshal Kray nor General Melas was equal to the task. Though both were brave soldiers, who had distinguished themselves in previous campaigns, neither had great military ability. In fact, the Archduke Charles was the only soldier in Austria capable of handling so large an army. He had already shown himself to be a great general. His views upon war were largely the outgrowth of his own successes. He was not wedded to the past. He saw the errors in the system of war so persistently advocated by the Aulic Council. He perceived the reasons for many of Bonaparte's previous successes. He had fought Bonaparte in Italy; and he comprehended, though somewhat dimly, Bonaparte's system of war. Moreover, his views upon the military situation were sound. Though he was far inferior to Bonaparte in military ability, yet, being the ablest soldier of Austria, he should have been made commander in chief of the Austrian armies, and should have been allowed to conduct the campaign in his own way. Probably he would not have succeeded against Bonaparte; and yet, who can say what the result would have been had he commanded one hundred and ninety thousand soldiers in the valley of the Danube? Austria was perishing for want of a leader, yet among her distinguished sons she saw not her ablest soldier.

Why was the Archduke Charles not made commander in chief? Why did Austria deprive herself of his services at the beginning of a great war? It was because the Aulic Council, which decided all military questions and directed the operations of the Austrian armies, did not approve of the Archduke's views upon the military situation. He had advised Austria to accept Bonaparte's offer of peace, and had pointed out that, in case of war, the principal effort against France should be made in the valley of the Danube. But the members of the Aulic Council knew little about military matters; they could see no merit in these suggestions. With a narrowness which they had many times exhibited before, they continued to blunder on, neither willing to take the advice of their only great soldier, nor able to comprehend the strategical combinations which their errors allowed Bonaparte to make. They originated faulty plans, sent unreliable information to the Austrian armies, and exercised over Melas and Kray a fatherly control which hampered them throughout the campaign. In short, they failed completely to appreciate the situation. "To the Aulic Council," said Jomini in 1804, "Austria owes all her reverses since the time of Prince Eugene of Savoy."

That the Aulic Council should fail was inevitable. In war the opinion of a trained soldier on military matters is worth more than that of a congress of a hundred men. Whenever the members of a senate, a council, or a congress, attempt to decide military questions, they are sure to err; for, being absent from the theatre of operations, they can neither see clearly the military situation, nor render decisions with promptness in critical times. Besides, their decisions are often halfway measures, neither one thing nor the other; like the laws passed by a bicameral legislature, they are nearly all compromises. In war there must be resolution, boldness, decision; to compromise is to court defeat.

In this chapter we have attempted to point out the strategical situation as it appeared to Bonaparte at the beginning of the campaign. In subsequent chapters we shall try to show how Bonaparte carried out some of his strategical conceptions; and how the operations of Masséna at Genoa, and of Moreau in the Black Forest, affected those of Bonaparte in Italy. Before closing the discussion, it will be well to remark that the most perfect strategy is of little value, unless it is executed with energy and culminates in victory. The difficulty lies not so much in the conception of great strategical projects, as in the execution of them. Strategy is only a means to an end. It does not win victories; but it clears the way for the winning of them, and adds to their value. It aims to bring a stronger force upon the battle-field, or to place an army in a position where victory will bring great results. But the battle must decide the struggle. " Even the weakest combatant does not lay down his arms to strategical manœuvres." It is victory upon the battle-field which settles the disputes of contending powers. There, amidst the clash of arms and the roar of cannon, amidst the shouts of triumph and the cries of despair, amidst the wounded, the dying, and the dead, victory decides the fate of armies and of empires.

CHAPTER II.

GENOA.[1]

IN the fertile valley of the Po, the Austrian army, commanded by Melas, found supplies in abundance for both men and animals. The equipment, discipline, and morale of the Austrians were good. The successes of the preceding year had encouraged them. They had that confidence in their commander so necessary to secure success. Filled with the enthusiasm of victory and looking hopefully forward to new triumphs, they were ready and anxious to be led against the French.

On the other hand, the Army of Italy, extending along the Apennines and Maritime Alps, found difficulty in obtaining supplies. Cut off from the productive basin of the Po by the Austrians on the north, and from the commerce of the sea by the British fleet on the south, this army had to depend almost entirely upon such supplies as could be sent from France over the Nice-Genoa road. The French soldiers were in a deplorable condition. Neglected by the French government, they were ragged, half-starved, discouraged. They had been defeated again and again. They lacked

[1] See Map 2.

the discipline and morale so essential to success.
A few soldiers had already deserted; many were
so emaciated that they could hardly bear arms,
and a number were sick with fever.

On assuming command of the Army of Italy,
Masséna took steps to improve the condition of
his men. With money furnished by Bonaparte
he supplied his troops with wheat, and by his
energetic measures soon brought about better
discipline. In Bonaparte's name, he published a
spirited proclamation, which did much to renew
the courage of his soldiers and to inspire in them
the hope of victory.

Notwithstanding the efforts of Masséna, his
soldiers were in a destitute condition. Only the
bare necessaries of life were furnished them.
Ammunition alone was sent them in abundance.
Though the Army of Italy numbered but forty
thousand men and was opposed to one hundred
and twenty thousand Austrians, Bonaparte would
not re-enforce it by a single soldier. In fact, all
the men and *matériel* collected in France were
used to strengthen Moreau's army and the Army
of Reserve. The Army of Italy was left to fight,
as best it could, a force overwhelmingly superior
in numbers, *matériel*, and equipment.

At the opening of the campaign, the condition of
the Army of Italy was such that but thirty-six thousand men were fit for active service. Of this force,
four thousand under Thurreau were in the Mont

Cenis Pass, so that there remained but thirty-two
thousand with which to hold the Apennines and
Maritime Alps from Genoa to the Col di Tenda.
Masséna's right wing, numbering eight thousand
under Miollis, held the fortified city of Genoa,
which, owing to the outlying works and natural
obstacles surrounding it, was an exceedingly strong
place; his centre, twelve thousand strong, commanded by Soult, defended the Bochetta Pass,
which opens upon Genoa, and the Cadibona Pass,
which opens upon Savona; his left, consisting of
twelve thousand under Suchet, occupied the Col
di Tenda, Nice, and the line of the Var.

Inasmuch as the active French army directly in
front of Melas numbered only thirty-two thousand
soldiers, and was spread out from Genoa to Nice,
he calculated that by directing twenty-five thousand men upon Genoa and a column of forty thousand upon the centre of the French line, he could
hold in check the French right, while he broke
through their centre and cut the Army of Italy in
two.   This feat accomplished, he expected that
his left wing of twenty-five thousand, with the aid
of the British fleet, would be able to enclose,
blockade, and capture Genoa, while his right wing
of forty thousand was forcing the remainder of the
Army of Italy across the Var.

On the French side, the plan of campaign that
offered the best results was one that Bonaparte
himself had originated.   He ordered Masséna to

leave only small detachments at the passes of
Tenda, Ormea, and Cadibona, and to concentrate
twenty-five or thirty thousand men at Genoa. In
written instructions to Masséna, the First Consul
set forth his views as follows : —

" Take care," said he, " not to extend your line too
widely. Put but few men on the Alps, or in the defile
of the Tenda, where the snow will protect you. Leave
some detachments around Nice and in the forts in its
vicinity ; keep four fifths of your force in Genoa and its
neighborhood. The enemy will debouch upon your
right in the direction of Genoa, on your centre in the
direction of Savona, and probably on the two points at
once. Refuse one of the two attacks, and throw yourself with all your forces united upon one of the enemy's
columns. The nature of the ground will not allow him
to avail himself of his superiority in artillery and cavalry ;
he can only attack you with his infantry, and yours is in-
finitely superior to his ; and, favored by the nature of the
place, it may make up for the deficiency in number. In
that broken country, if you manœuvre well, with 30,000
men you may give battle to 60,000. In order to carry
60,000 light-armed troops into Liguria, Melas must have
90,000, which supposes a total army of 120,000 at least.
Melas possesses neither your talents nor activity ; you have
no reason to fear him. If he appear in the direction of
Nice, you being at Genoa, let him come on, stir not from
your position ; he will not advance far if you remain in
Liguria, ready to throw yourself upon his rear, or upon
the troops left in Piedmont."

Though this plan was excellent for holding in
check the Austrians for a time, unfortunately it

was beyond the execution of Masséna. Provisions were so scarce in Genoa that it would have been foolish to concentrate nearly the whole of the Army of Italy there. To feed his army was the difficulty that confronted Masséna. For this reason he scattered his troops along the Apennines, and occupied the seaboard from Genoa to Nice. In this position, his soldiers could seize the meagre supplies that the barren country afforded, and could more easily obtain provisions direct from France. Though it is doubtful whether Masséna fully appreciated the advantages of Bonaparte's plan, nevertheless, he would probably have carried it out, had he not been prevented from doing so by a lack of provisions, and by the beginning of hostilities much earlier than either he or Bonaparte expected.

On the 5th of April, Melas, leaving thirty-five thousand Austrians under General Kaim to occupy the fortresses of northwestern Italy and to watch the passes of the Alps, advanced with sixty-five thousand[1] to attack Masséna. His forces were divided into three columns: General Ott with fifteen thousand men ascended the Trebbia and presented himself before the defiles of the mountains which shoot off from the main chain of the Apennines and extend along the east side of

[1] In addition to the forces of Melas mentioned above, twenty thousand Austrians were scattered throughout northern Italy, several thousand of whom were in Tuscany, in the Papal States, and in the fortress of Mantua.

Genoa; General Hohenzollern with ten thousand marched upon the Bochetta Pass on the north side of the city; and Melas himself with forty thousand ascended the Bormida, and attacked the forces of Soult and Suchet along the Apennines and Maritime Alps. Confining his principal attack to the centre of the French line, Melas succeeded, after hard fighting, in forcing his way through the Cadibona Pass, which movement cut in two the Army of Italy and separated Soult from Suchet. The former fell back towards Genoa; the latter, towards Nice. In these engagements both sides fought fiercely. Though the French had the advantage of position, they were compelled to give way before the onslaughts of superior numbers.

At the Bochetta Pass, the attack made by General Hohenzollern was repulsed; but on the east side of Genoa the French, numbering less than four thousand, could not hold the defiles and crest of the Apennines against General Ott's force of fifteen thousand. The Austrians drove the French across the mountains, then surrounded and invested the French forts that protected the city on that side. By this successful attack, General Ott gained a foothold within cannon-shot of the walls of Genoa.

Thus far Melas had been successful. The first great step in his undertaking had been accomplished. Now he could close in upon Masséna with his left wing, force him back into Genoa, and hold him there as in a vise; while with his right, strongly re-enforced, he could advance against Suchet, perhaps crush him or drive him across the Var into France.

Meanwhile Masséna was in a precarious situation. His army was cut in two; his communications with France were severed. In the face of superior numbers, Suchet was being driven back towards Nice, and Soult was withdrawing the shattered remains of his forces towards Genoa. In front of the city and along the Italian shore, the British fleet was actively supporting the operations of Melas. On the east side of the city, the Austrians had gained the crests of the mountains; and at the Bochetta Pass they were ready to make another attack, which would prove successful. In fact, Masséna was surrounded. The allies were closing in upon him. Already their guns could be heard at Genoa; soon they might force him inside the walls of the city.

But it was the want of provisions that gave Masséna the greatest anxiety. Food was already scarce, and there was but little hope of receiving any more. Though defeat and famine were staring him in the face, yet he did not allow himself to be discouraged. He realized that it was his duty to maintain a stubborn resistance, and to engage actively as many of the Austrians as possible, in order that Bonaparte could cross the

Alps and strike the Austrian rear. By prolonging the conflict he would gain time ; and time was of the greatest importance to the success of Bonaparte.

In order to understand how Masséna attempted to carry out his purposes, it is necessary to describe briefly the situation of Genoa and its fortifications. The city lies at the foot of a spur of the Apennines, on the shore of the gulf that bears its name. This spur, running south from the main chain towards the sea, divides into two ridges which extend to the water's edge, one along the east side, the other along the west side of the city. Upon the crests of the ridges, which form two sides of a triangle, having its base on the sea, a number of forts had been constructed and were occupied by the French. Within the triangle was the walled city of Genoa, containing about one hundred thousand inhabitants. Thus the city had two lines of fortifications surrounding it : one along the ridges and crests of the Apennines, the other along the walls of the city.

Masséna had but eighteen thousand soldiers to defend Genoa. But with this force in so strongly fortified a place, he knew that he could hold out as long as his provisions lasted. Perhaps, by vigorous fighting, he might be able to unite with Suchet, and in this way re-establish his communications with France.

For the purpose of carrying out these views,

Masséna resolved to drive the Austrians from the crest of the Apennines on the east side of the city; then, if possible, to effect a junction with Suchet by a movement along the Genoa-Nice road. Accordingly, on the 7th of April, at the head of a strong force, he issued from the city and vigorously attacked General Ott. The French drove the Austrians from the crest of the Apennines, and, after desperate fighting, seized and reoccupied the Austrian positions.

Having been successful in this attack, Masséna then made preparations for a movement towards Nice. For this purpose, he divided his command into two parts: he left Miollis with eight thousand men to defend Genoa; and with the remaining ten thousand, divided into two columns, one of which was commanded by Soult, the other by himself, he began his westward march. At the same time, Suchet, who had been informed of Masséna's plan, marched eastward from Nice to attack the Austrians from that side. Both Masséna and Suchet met with fierce opposition. Neither could make much headway against the overwhelming forces of Melas. For several days the fighting was furious, desperate, and bloody. Though Masséna captured several thousand Austrians, he was finally repulsed and driven back. On the 18th of April he re-entered Genoa; and Suchet again fell back towards the Var.

Masséna was now enclosed in the city. From

this time dates the beginning of the siege of Genoa, — one of the most memorable and stubbornly contested struggles mentioned in history. In this brief account of these operations, we shall not attempt to describe the sufferings of the French soldiers who fought and starved and died here; nor to dwell upon the heroic deeds of their commander, — as stubborn a soldier and fierce a fighter as ever trod a battle-field; but rather to point out the important facts that had a bearing upon the operations of Bonaparte, and to show why Masséna, in the midst of a starving army and a starving city, still continued to fight on.

The Army of Italy having been cut in two, Melas gave orders that General Ott should take command of the thirty thousand Austrians then surrounding Genoa, and, if possible, force Masséna to capitulate; and that General Elsnitz, with twenty-five thousand, should proceed vigorously against Suchet, whose active force at this time numbered but ten thousand men. Masséna himself had but fifteen thousand; but nevertheless he had resolved to hold out to the last extremity. He sent an aid-de-camp to the First Consul to apprise him of the situation of the Army of Italy, and to urge him to hasten the movement of the Army of Reserve. Realizing that the scarcity of provisions would prevent a long resistance, Masséna took possession of all the wheat he could find in the city. Even the grain of inferior quality, such as rye and oats, was seized and made into bread. Though the quantity of bread thus obtained was small, and the quality poor, it sufficed to keep alive the soldiers and the poor of Genoa during the first two weeks of the siege. But ten days passed, and the supply of bread was almost exhausted. Moreover, its bad quality was already causing sickness. A number of soldiers were in the hospitals; and many were so weak and emaciated that they could hardly bear the weight of their arms.

Though the outlook was gloomy to Masséna's soldiers, some hope yet remained in his rugged soul. Perhaps a storm or adverse winds might drive the English fleet off the Italian shore, and thus allow the French ships to bring in provisions; perhaps Bonaparte, now that he understood the situation, would hurry across the Alps into Italy, and strike a blow that would cause Melas to raise the siege of Genoa and set free Masséna's perishing army.

Masséna's force, exclusive of the sick, now numbered but twelve thousand men; part of whom were occupying the outlying works, and the remainder, within the city, were acting as a reserve. His purpose was to attack the Austrians, whenever they advanced towards the city, and to exhaust them as much as possible by partial engagements. By this means he expected to prevent Melas from sending away a force, either to aid the Austrians in front of Suchet, or to oppose the projected march of Bonaparte across the Alps.

On the 30th of April General Ott, supported by English gun-boats in the Gulf of Genoa, made simultaneous attacks on the east, north, and west sides of the city. In these attacks, he met with considerable success. On all three sides the Austrian columns advanced and occupied more favorable positions. In fact, they gained the crests of several mountain ridges within cannon-shot of the city, and succeeded in capturing several French forts.

Masséna fought fiercely. Throwing his reserve first on one side of the city and then on the other, in order to re-enforce his troops occupying the out-lying works, he finally forced back the Austrians from their commanding positions and recovered the lost forts. The success of Masséna at this time was discouraging to General Ott; for he knew that he could not lay close siege to the place until his troops gained the crests of the Apennines and invested, or captured, the outlying works.

Meanwhile the twenty-five thousand Austrians under Elsnitz had, by vigorous fighting, driven Suchet from position to position. They had even forced him to abandon Nice, and to fall back on the Var. On this river, which had been strongly fortified, Suchet rallied his scattered forces. Having received from the departments of southern France a considerable re-enforcement, which increased his total strength to fourteen thousand men, he was able, in this position, to make a successful stand, and to stop the onward rush of the victorious Austrians.

As soon as Bonaparte learned of the hopeless condition of affairs at Genoa, he saw the necessity of hurrying across the Alps with the Army of Reserve. But since the successful execution of his plan depended upon his receiving a large re-enforcement from the Army of the Rhine, and since Moreau could not safely detach this force till he had defeated Kray and pushed him back from Lake Constance, Bonaparte was compelled to delay his own movement. Moreau was slow to begin; and his lingering inactivity gave Bonaparte intense anxiety, for it not only paralyzed the operations of the Army of Reserve, but prolonged the sufferings of the Army of Italy. Repeatedly Bonaparte urged Moreau to cross the Rhine and attack Kray. " Hasten," said the First Consul, " hasten by your success to accelerate the arrival of the moment at which Masséna can be disengaged. That general wants provisions. For fifteen days he has been enduring with his debilitated soldiers a struggle of despair. Your patriotism is addressed, your self-interest ; for if Masséna shall be compelled to capitulate, it will be necessary to take from you a part of your forces, for the purpose of hurrying down the Rhone, in order to assist the departments of the south."

Finally, on the 25th of April, Moreau began his advance against Kray. It is not the intention at this time to describe in detail these operations. At present it is sufficient to say that Moreau executed vigorously his part in Bonaparte's great plan. Having defeated Kray in two battles, he detached, on the 11th of May, a corps of fifteen thousand men from his army, gave the command of it to General Moncey, and ordered him to march by way of the St. Gothard into Italy.

The time had come for Bonaparte to move forward the Army of Reserve. Accordingly, on the 15th of May, he began his advance by way of the Great St. Bernard into Italy. While this army of forty thousand and this corps of fifteen thousand are marching hopefully forward across the Alps, from France and Germany respectively, let us again turn our attention to Masséna, who, amidst famine and death, is desperately fighting on.

On the 5th of May a small vessel, containing grain sufficient to last the besieged garrison for five days, ran the blockade and entered Genoa. Masséna felt encouraged, and shortly afterwards made a sortie on the east side of the city. Though he drove the Austrians from their positions, this assault was the last of his successes. On the 13th of May he attempted another assault, but was badly defeated. Henceforth his soldiers were so weak that they lacked the strength to undertake any movement beyond the walls of Genoa. In fact, many, not being able to bear the weight of their arms, were compelled to sit down while doing guard duty. Consequently, Masséna was obliged to limit his efforts to the defence of the city, and to the task of providing food for his men.

By the 20th of May the bread and meat were exhausted; even the horses had all been consumed. All the linseed, starch, and cacao found in the city were then collected and made into a kind of bread, which was all but indigestible. This wretched and repulsive food, and a soup made of herbs were all that remained to sustain life. Nevertheless, Masséna would not capitulate. Stubborn and courageous to the last, he seemed bent on defying even starvation and death. Possibly Bonaparte might yet come; for word had been brought that he had crossed the Alps. It was reported that, on the 20th of May, his army had been seen descending the Great St. Bernard into Italy. If so, why did he not come? It was now the 30th of May, and not another word had been heard of him. Could he have met with defeat? Could he, whose movements were usually so rapid, whose blows were so terrible and unexpected — could he have been ten days in Italy, and not yet have struck the blow that was to shatter the Austrian rear and bring relief to Masséna's perishing soldiers?

With intense anxiety these despairing men looked for the coming of Bonaparte. But he came

not. Already discouraged, they now lost all hope.
A few went so far as to destroy their arms. Some
plotted; others talked wildly of the sufferings and
horrors that they were called upon to endure. All
urged Masséna to surrender; but he would not
yield. He begged his soldiers to hold out a little
longer. He told them that the First Consul was
advancing to their relief; that if they capitulated
now, they would lose the results of all their heroism, all their sufferings. "Yet a few days," said
he, "nay, a few hours, and you will be delivered."

Thus, for a brief time, Masséna succeeded
in raising the hopes of his soldiers. Again
they looked expectantly towards the Apennines.
Never was anxiety more intense. In every sound,
in every echo, in every flash of light along the
northern horizon, they thought that they saw signs
of the coming of Bonaparte. But they were mis-
taken. Despair seized them; no hope remained.
Even Masséna saw that the end had come; for the
last ounce of that wretched food composed of linseed, starch, and cacao, had been consumed. It
was now absolutely necessary to surrender. Yet
Masséna's inflexible nature would not wholly yield.
He declared that he would never capitulate, unless
his soldiers should be allowed to march out with
the honors of war, and with the liberty to fight
again when beyond the enemy's line. And he
kept his resolution. The Austrians were compelled to accept these terms.

That the reader may understand why General Ott did not continue the struggle a few days longer, and thus force Masséna to surrender unconditionally, let us consider for a moment the situation at this time in the valley of the Po.

On the 2d of June, two days before Masséna capitulated, Bonaparte entered Milan, and there awaited Moncey's corps, which did not arrive till the 6th of June.

On the 29th of May Melas learned that Bonaparte was advancing on Milan. On the 31st he learned that Moreau had defeated Kray, and that Moncey's corps was marching by way of the St. Gothard into Italy. At once he comprehended the vast plan of the First Consul. Melas was in consternation; he had been surprised. To him the Army of Reserve was no longer imaginary; it was a reality. Moreover, it was rapidly approaching a favorable position from which it could strike a formidable blow at the Austrian communications. Melas saw the necessity of concentrating immediately his scattered forces. He must, if possible, break through the French Army before it closed in upon him. Accordingly, on the 31st of May, he sent orders to General Elsnitz to quit the Var and march on Alessandria; and instructed General Ott to raise the siege of Genoa and hasten north in order to defend the line of the Po.

General Ott received this order on the 2d of June, during the negotiations for the capitulation of Genoa. He realized that he must either raise at once the siege of the city or else accept Masséna's terms.

On the 4th of June Masséna surrendered. On the 5th his active force, numbering eight thousand men, set out over the Genoa-Nice road to join Suchet, who at this time was following closely upon the rear of the Austrians in his front, as they withdrew towards Alessandria. In addition to his active force, Masséna surrendered four thousand sick soldiers at Genoa; but it was stipulated that they should be cared for, and upon their recovery should be sent back to join the French army. Having made these arrangements, Masséna himself proceeded by sea to join Suchet.

During these operations the English fleet in the Gulf of Genoa actively supported the Austrians; but the English corps in Minorca remained inactive. No effort was made to land it either at Genoa or at any other point along the Italian or French coast.

During these engagements the fighting on both sides was desperate, the loss heavy. In prisoners, killed, and wounded, the Austrians lost about twenty thousand; the French, about fourteen thousand. But the loss of the latter was in reality much greater; for out of Masséna's active force of eight thousand that had marched out of Genoa to join Suchet, probably six thousand were unfit for arduous service. The total number, therefore, on the French side put *hors de combat*, for the time being, may be reckoned at about twenty thousand men.

The active operations of the Army of Italy were ended. They had begun on the 5th of April, and had terminated on the 4th of June. For two months Masséna had shown himself firm as a rock, — had gloriously performed his part in Bonaparte's great plan.

COMMENTS.

AT the outset the Austrian forces were greatly scattered. A few thousand were in Tuscany and in the Papal States; an Austrian garrison was occupying the fortress of Mantua, which is situated on the Mincio about twenty miles south of Lake Garda; twenty-five thousand were moving forward in two columns to attack Genoa; forty thousand were being directed on the Apennines and Maritime Alps; and thirty-five thousand were occupying the fortresses of northwestern Italy, and guarding the Italian entrances to the passes of the Alps.

The purpose of Melas was to push forward across the Apennines and Maritime Alps, force the line of the Var, and invade France. How best to accomplish this project was the problem before him. Having an army of one hundred and twenty thousand soldiers and being opposed to but forty thousand, he believed that his force was sufficiently large to undertake the invasion of France. Since the French line directly in his front extended along the mountains from Genoa to the Col di Tenda, Melas could easily overwhelm the French centre and cut the Army of Italy in two; then, by leaving a sufficient force to surround Genoa, he could push forward vigorously to the Var with the bulk of his forces, and perhaps carry the position there before the French had time to make the necessary dispositions for defending it. Had he adopted this plan, and made arrangements with Admiral Keith and General Abercromby to have the English corps in Minorca landed at the same time on the coast of Italy or France, he would doubtless have been successful.

He was not successful because he did not thoroughly appreciate the situation. He did not know how to handle his army. He scattered his forces, and thus dissipated his strength. He spent too much energy at Genoa, and not enough along the Var. His rear guard, which consisted of the thirty-five thousand soldiers under General Kaim in Piedmont, and of twenty thousand scattered throughout Italy, was unnecessarily large, and yet was so divided, subdivided, and dispersed that it was weak at all points. In short, Melas committed many errors.

First: In advancing against Genoa with twenty-five thousand men, divided into two columns, and against the centre of the French line with a third column of forty thousand, Melas gave to Masséna the opportunity of holding in check with small forces two of the columns, while he concentrated his remaining forces against the third. In fact, this was exactly what Masséna did. He left eight thousand soldiers in and around Genoa to hold the place, then united the rest of his troops near Savona to attack Melas. When it is remembered that these three Austrian columns of attack were separated by impassable obstacles, and could not support one another, the errors of Melas become apparent to every soldier. That, in spite of such errors, he was successful in cutting the Army of Italy in two and in gaining the crest of the mountains on the east side of Genoa was due to his great superiority in numbers. His attacking force numbered sixty-five thousand men, while Masséna had but thirty-two thousand.

In this connection it is worthy of notice that numbers alone can neutralize and finally overcome any advantage of position or of generalship. Thus mediocrity may triumph over genius. Even a Napoleon cannot conquer in the face of odds sufficiently great. At Leipsic one hundred and fifty thousand soldiers, commanded by him, were defeated by two hundred and ninety thousand allies. In the Waterloo campaign, which, from a strategical point of view, is a masterpiece in generalship, his army of one hundred and twenty-five thousand men was crushed and overwhelmed by the armies of England and Prussia, numbering two hundred and eighteen thousand soldiers. Hence follows the first principle of war: *Be as strong as possible at the vital point.*

Second: A victory on the Var was of much greater importance to Melas than was the capitulation of Genoa; for should this river be once forced, there would be no further obstacle to the invasion of France; and, besides, a successful attack on Suchet would hopelessly deprive Masséna of all support, and would in time force him to surrender. In truth, the great effort for success should have been made on the Var. But Melas failed to appreciate this fact. After he had separated Masséna from Suchet by forcing the centre of the French line, he directed his greatest efforts to the capture of Genoa. For this purpose the troops surrounding the place were increased to thirty thousand men, and were kept at or about this strength till Masséna surrendered; while on the Var the Austrian forces actively engaged during these operations numbered but twenty-five thousand. Since, at the outset, Masséna had only eighteen thousand combatants at Genoa, and since this number was rapidly reduced from day to day by casualties and sickness, it is evident that Melas could have surrounded the place and have maintained the siege there with less than thirty thousand soldiers. The increase of his troops beyond the number necessary to hold securely the place was injudicious; for the surplus could have been used with greater effect on the Var. Moreover, the surplus did not hasten the surrender of Masséna; for he was able to hold out against thirty thousand till his provisions were exhausted. Against ten thousand less he could have held out no longer. Again and again Melas assaulted the works surrounding the city, but his efforts were, to a great extent, a waste of energy; for they resulted in a greater loss to the Austrians than to the French, and had little or no effect in hastening the surrender of Masséna.

In the treatment of fortresses, it is worth while to compare the methods of Bonaparte with those of Melas. In the Italian campaign of 1796–97, the strong fortresses which were held by the allies, and which were on the direct line of Bonaparte's operations, did not stop his progress for a moment. Though from a lack of siege artillery, he could not completely invest them, he pushed forward past them to decide, if possible, their fate upon the open battle-field. In that campaign he invested the fortress of Mantua, containing twelve thousand combatants, with ten thousand men; and though the besieged were finally increased to twenty thousand soldiers, he continued with ten thousand or less to hold them in check for seven months, while he won the battles of Lonato, Castiglione, Roveredo, Bassano, San Georgio, Arcole, and Rivoli. "It is upon the open field of battle," said Napoleon, "that the fate of fortresses and empires is decided."

Third: The Austrian rear guard was unnecessarily large. It consisted of fifty-five thousand soldiers. At present it is not the purpose to point out in detail the errors that Melas committed by leaving so large a force inactive in Italy, but rather to show that this force was larger than necessary, and that the surplus troops composing it could have been used to much greater advantage along the Var. The necessity for a strong rear guard in northwestern Italy becomes apparent when it is remembered that Thurreau was occupying the Mont Cenis Pass with four thousand men, and might at any time attempt to issue therefrom upon the flank and rear of Melas as he advanced towards the Var. Inasmuch as Thurreau's detachment occupied a favorable position from which to attack the Austrians, it was necessary, perhaps, that Melas should leave ten or twelve thousand men to hold this force in check. There was, too, some likelihood that French troops might issue into Italy from Switzerland by the St. Gothard Pass or the Simplon; a few thousand troops were therefore needed in that vicinity to give warning in case the French attempted to enter Italy from that direction. At this time Melas doubted the existence of the Army of Reserve; but, had he believed it to be a reality, doubtless he would not have expected Bonaparte to cross the Great St. Bernard. And even had he expected him from that direction, perhaps no better arrangement of his rear guard could have been made than to leave five thousand men before the St. Gothard, five thousand before the Great St. Bernard, and twenty thousand near Turin with their left flank well extended towards the Mont Cenis Pass. In this central position the rear guard could march rapidly to attack the French, should they enter Italy by any one of these passes, and could hold them in check till a larger Austrian force could be concentrated. Had Melas known that Bonaparte expected to cross the Alps with the Army of Reserve, no better method could have been devised to prevent the projected march of Bonaparte than to force the Var and invade France. This undertaking being accomplished, there would be no further danger of Bonaparte's crossing the Alps; for he must then fight on the west side of the mountains to save France from invasion. The surest way to protect the Austrian rear was to force the Var. Every spare man should have been directed there. Twenty thousand could have held Genoa; thirty thousand would have sufficed for a rear guard; and of the remaining seventy thousand, probably fifty or sixty thousand could have united in an attack upon Suchet.

Fourth: Had the English corps of twelve thousand men been thrown upon the coast of France just in rear of Suchet, while sixty thousand Austrians were attacking him in front, who can doubt what the result would have been? Suchet had but fourteen thousand men; and against such overwhelming odds he would have been compelled to yield.

With a large and brave army, capable of doing great things, if it had been properly led, Melas so scattered it and dissipated his strength that he virtually accomplished nothing. Though he commanded one hundred and twenty thousand men, he brought but twenty-five thousand upon the vital point. In short, he committed blunder upon blunder, and finally failed in his undertaking.

The problem before Masséna was to hold in check the Austrians in Italy until Bonaparte could perfect his arrangements, cross the Alps, and strike the Austrian rear. Masséna could not expect to do more than this; for he could not take the offensive single-handed against an Austrian army three times the size of his own. Moreover, he was in possession of the strong defensive positions of Genoa, of the Apennines and Maritime Alps, and of the line of the Var, where inferior numbers could make a vigorous resistance against greatly superior forces. Masséna could not know how soon Bonaparte would cross the Alps. His object, therefore, was so to arrange his troops as to enable them to hold out as long as possible.

At the outset of the campaign the Army of Italy

was stationed as follows: eight thousand were at Genoa; twelve thousand, in the vicinity of Savona; twelve thousand, at the Tenda Pass, at Nice, and along the Var; and four thousand, in the Mont Cenis Pass. By examining the several positions on the map, it will be seen that the French forces were greatly scattered. Thirty-two thousand, under the direct command of Masséna, were defending the line of the Apennines and Maritime Alps from Genoa to the Col di Tenda, a distance of about seventy-five miles; and four thousand, under Thurreau, were holding the Mont Cenis Pass, which lies in the French Alps about one hundred and twenty miles north of Nice.

Inasmuch as the direct road from Italy into France crossed the Alps over this pass, it was necessary to leave Thurreau's detachment there. Otherwise an Austrian corps of several thousand could have crossed the Alps at this point, thence have marched south along the west side of the mountains, and have attacked the French on the Var in rear, while Melas with his main forces was advancing across the Apennines to attack them in front. Moreover, in this favorable position, Thurreau, unless strongly opposed, could descend the Alps and fall upon the flank and rear of the Austrians as they advanced towards Nice. It was necessary, therefore, for Melas to leave ten or twelve thousand soldiers of the Austrian rear guard near the Italian entrance to the Mont Cenis Pass in order to hold Thurreau in check. Thus, though this French detachment could take no active part in the engagements along the Apennines and Maritime Alps, its four thousand men did good service in the struggle by rendering nugatory the fighting power of a much larger Austrian force.

Since the French along the Apennines and Maritime Alps occupied a front of about seventy-five miles in extent, they could not concentrate rapidly. Consequently, Melas could throw a strong force against some point of their long line with great hope of success. In fact, by attacking the centre of their line with superior numbers, he could cut the Army of Italy in two. Having in this way separated Masséna from Suchet, Melas could concentrate an overwhelming force against each in succession, and thus defeat them separately. Moreover, this movement would cut the communications of Masséna with France, and compel him to seek safety in Genoa, where the opposition of superior numbers and the scarcity of provisions must eventually force him to surrender.

Strategically, therefore, the situation of the Army of Italy was faulty; yet it must be remembered that the lack of provisions was the principal cause that led Masséna to adopt this plan. In order better to subsist his troops, he had scattered them. But was there no other course that offered him greater advantages? A discussion of the subject should throw light on this question.

First: He might have left detachments to hold the Cadibona and Ormea passes, and have concentrated the bulk of his army in rear of the Tenda Pass in the vicinity of Nice. Had he adopted this course, his troops would have been united, and could have drawn their provisions direct from France. But no other advantages would have resulted. With the French in this position, Melas could have attacked the passes of the Apennines in force, and have gained possession of the Genoa-Nice road; which operation would have compelled Masséna to fall back on the Var. There he might have been able to make a successful stand for a time. But should the Austrians once force this position, there would be no further obstacle to the invasion of France. To adopt this plan would undoubtedly have been a mistake; for it involved the abandonment of Genoa, which was so strong, both naturally and artificially, that a small force could hold it for a long time against superior numbers. Moreover, in a defensive campaign, when the odds are greatly in favor of the attacking army, and when the object is to gain time, advantage should be taken of every strong position.

Second: Masséna might have left small detachments to hold the passes of the Apennines and Maritime Alps, and have concentrated the rest of his army at Genoa. Indeed this was the plan that Bonaparte had ordered Masséna to carry out; but

it presented great difficulties. Provisions were
scarce at Genoa. Had Masséna increased his
strength there to thirty thousand soldiers, starvation and disease would sooner have done their
deadly work. Moreover, the greater fighting
power thus obtained would have availed him
nothing; for with half the number he in fact held
the city till the food was exhausted. Had Masséna adopted this course, undoubtedly he must
have surrendered at least three weeks earlier. In
that case, the Austrians would have crossed the
Var into France, and Bonaparte would have abandoned his march into Italy. In that case, the decisive struggle between Melas and Bonaparte would
doubtless have taken place in the valley of the
Rhone instead of in the valley of the Po. Indeed,
it is not improbable to assume that, had Masséna
attempted to carry out either one of the plans
mentioned, Bonaparte would have been obliged
to change the entire conduct of the campaign. In
war small matters often determine great events.

Under the circumstances then existing, Masséna
was justified in not carrying out Bonaparte's instructions; nevertheless, had he fully appreciated
the advantages of the plan, he would undoubtedly have made a greater effort to collect supplies
at Genoa. Inasmuch as he took command of the
Army of Italy before the arrival of the British
fleet in the Gulf of Genoa, possibly he might
have shipped sufficient grain from Toulon to

supply the Army of Italy during a siege of several
months. For the purpose of this discussion, let
us assume that he had done so; and that, in accordance with Bonaparte's orders, he had left a
few thousand men to hold the passes of the Apennines and Maritime Alps, and had collected about
thirty thousand at Genoa. What would have been
the result? What are the advantages of this situation? Surely, they are many; for Bonaparte
himself originated the plan.

Since the mountains and outlying works surrounding Genoa made it a veritable stronghold,
Bonaparte calculated that the Army of Italy could
maintain itself there against greatly outnumbering
forces; and that the Austrians would hardly dare
to force the Apennines and push forward in order
to invade France while thirty thousand men remained undefeated in their rear. In this position,
too, Masséna could, at any time, leave a small
force to hold Genoa, then march rapidly westward along the south side of the Apennines, and
arrive before any one of the threatened passes
with almost his entire army; or should the Austrians force the Apennines and advance towards
France, he could fall upon their flank and rear,
and perhaps sever their communications, while
his own communications with Genoa would be
protected by the mountains on one side and by
the sea on the other. In fact, this position would
enable him to take advantage of the topography

of the country to the fullest extent. If he should make an attack in force upon the Austrians from one of the passes in his possession, the mountains would protect him during his concentration, and would give strength to his position after his forces had united. If he should remain at Genoa, the fortifications and natural obstacles there would increase enormously his fighting power. It is evident, too, that he might march out of the city, force his way through the Apennines, and cut the communications of the Austrians in the valley of the Po. If, while holding the Apennines, he should advance with his main army over the Genoa-Nice road to attack the Austrians, he would be in a position where a victory would bring him great results, and where a defeat would do him but little harm. Should he be successful, he could sever the Austrian communications and perhaps ruin their army; should he be repulsed, he could fall back and seek safety in Genoa. " If," says Bonaparte in his instructions to Masséna, " Melas appear in the direction of Nice, you being at Genoa, let him come on, stir not from your position: he will not advance far if you remain in Liguria, ready to throw yourself upon his rear, or upon the troops left in Piedmont."

In short, Bonaparte's design was so to make use of the works of nature and of art as to prolong the conflict and increase the effectiveness of Masséna's small army. Thus it was that Bonaparte expected thirty thousand French to defeat sixty thousand Austrians. Thus it was that he expected the Army of Italy to hold out against overwhelming odds till he himself could strike the decisive blow.

Though from a strategical point of view the plan set forth in Bonaparte's instructions to Masséna possessed many advantages, yet it had one great defect. With the main bulk of Masséna's forces concentrated at Genoa, and with small detachments holding the line of the Apennines and Maritime Alps, it is evident that Melas could force his way across the mountains between Genoa and the Tenda Pass, and thus cut the communications of Masséna and enclose him in Genoa. It is evident, too, that Melas could surround Masséna and eventually force him to capitulate. The French might fight desperately and hold out for months; yet, in time, they would be compelled to yield. The histories of wars and of sieges show that, when a commander allows himself to be enclosed in a fortification, he is doomed to defeat in the end. "*Great armies,*" says Von der Goltz, "*which are shut up in a fortress after lost battles, are, as the history of investments from Alesia down to Metz proves, almost always lost.*" Again he says: "Among all the relations between fortress and field army, the latter must make it a supreme rule *never to allow itself to be thrown into a fortress.* Even to pass through it is dangerous, because the army may be kept prisoner there against its will. *Fortresses protect the troops they contain, but, at the same time, anchor them to the spot. An army can easily be got behind fortifications, but only with difficulty back again into the open field, unless it be that strong help from without lends it a hand."* When the commander of an army is hard pressed, and there is near at hand a strongly fortified place with outlying works of great strength, and provisions and water within, the temptation is great to seek security there. Second rate generals accept such opportunities, but in doing so they make fatal mistakes. The great masters of the art of war manœuvre for position, and become themselves the besiegers, or decide upon the open battle-field the fate of their fortresses and their armies.

During all Napoleon's military operations he never allowed himself to be besieged in any place. How, then, are we to reconcile this fact with the instructions that he sent to Masséna? Why should he order Masséna to take up a position which would allow his army to be besieged, and finally to be captured or destroyed? To answer satisfactorily these questions, it is necessary to consider the operations of Masséna in connection with the projected operations of Bonaparte. The Army of Italy was essentially a containing force. Its duty was to hold Melas in check for a time. How Masséna could best *prolong* the conflict was the

problem that Bonaparte was solving. That the
Army of Italy should finally be defeated was of
small consequence; that it should not be defeated
before Bonaparte had time to effect the destruction of Melas was of great consequence. If it
could hold out till then, the victory of Bonaparte
over Melas would render nugatory the triumph of
Melas over Masséna. If it could hold out till then,
the success of Melas at Genoa would avail him
nothing; for it would be swallowed up by a
greater success, which was destined to produce
far greater results.

Bonaparte believed that Masséna was strong
enough to hold Melas in check; and since every
spare man was needed to strengthen Moreau's
army and the Army of Reserve, he would not send
any re-enforcements to the Army of Italy. Doubtless an ordinary general would have marched the
entire Army of Reserve to the support of Masséna.
What would have been the result? With only
eighty thousand Frenchmen to oppose one hundred and twenty thousand Austrians, there would
have been a long struggle in Italy. Guided by
the genius of Bonaparte the French might have
repeated the successes of 1796–97; but even had
they done so, months of hard fighting would have
been necessary in order to drive the Austrians out
of northern Italy. In the Marengo campaign Bonaparte expected to accomplish as great results in
less time. The struggle for the mastery was to

take place, not along the Apennines, but in the valley of the Po. Thus it was that no re-enforcements were sent to Masséna, and that little or nothing was done to improve the condition of the Army of Italy. "It must be admitted," says Thiers, "that the army of Liguria [1] was treated a little as a sacrificed army. Not a man was sent to it. Materials of war only were supplied to it; and even under that head such only as were absolutely needful. It was in a different direction that the great efforts of the government were exerted, because it was in a different direction that the great blows were to be dealt. The army of Liguria was exposed to destruction in order to gain the time which should render the others victorious. Such is the hard necessity of war, which passes over the heads of these to strike the heads of those; obliging those to die that these may live and conquer."

It seems hard that Masséna's soldiers should have starved and died, and no help have been sent them. It seems hard that they should have struggled on, performing heroic deeds, with little or no hope of victory. But such is war; some must fail in order that others may triumph. In beleaguered Genoa, at the bridge of Arcole, amid the snows of Russia, men must die. But do they die in vain? Perhaps so: and yet, who shall say?

[1] In the "History of the Consulate and Empire" by Thiers, he often refers to the Army of Italy as the "army of Liguria."

Victory was Bonaparte's object; and to obtain it, he would, if necessary, sacrifice the Army of Italy. He had an eye for great results. His glance penetrated the most complicated military problems. It was his merit that he knew how, with the forces at hand, to do great things. He did not fritter away his strength by sending useless detachments here and there. The four thousand men under Thurreau were a necessity in the Mont Cenis Pass; the Army of Italy, with Masséna at its head, was large enough, but not too large, to do the work expected of it; and the Army of Reserve, re-enforced by a corps of Moreau's army, was of sufficient strength to produce the desired effect at the vital point. Even Genoa, the Alps, and the Apennines were made to serve Bonaparte. Nature was his re-enforcement. Like a mighty tide he moved on, neither deterred by the sufferings of the Army of Italy, nor stopped by the great chain of the Alps.

He who would censure Bonaparte for not marching to the relief of Masséna must remember that such a course would have prolonged the struggle and ultimately would have led to a greater destruction of life. Yet humane considerations probably did not influence his decisions one iota. Let us not, then, attribute to him the virtues of a Lincoln; but let us set forth with fairness what he did and why he did it. We may not admire the man who can thus sacrifice an army to attain his ends; but

we must admire the soldier who penetrates the
future, who sees what to do and how to do it, who
bends every energy to the accomplishment of the
task, and with relentless purpose, turning neither
to the right hand nor to the left, marches on to
victory.

CHAPTER III.

MOREAU IN GERMANY.[1]

LYING in the angle of the Rhine between Lake Constance and Strasburg is a mountainous region known as the Black Forest, which takes its name from the dark foliage of its pine timber. The general shape of the Black Forest is that of a triangle; its base resting on the Rhine between Lake Constance and Bâle, and its apex pointing north. Its total length is ninety-three miles; its breadth varies from forty-six to thirteen miles, and its average elevation is about three thousand feet. On the south and west sides the mountains are rugged and steep, but on the east side they descend gradually to the lower level of the adjacent country.

Within its limits the Black Forest presents an almost impassable barrier to an army attempting to enter Germany from France. A few roads lead through it; but they lie in the fissures of the mountains, and are therefore difficult for the passage of troops. Extending into the Black Forest opposite Strasburg is the Kinzig Valley, and oppo-

[1] See Map 3.

site Brisach are the Höllenthal (valley of Hell) and the valley of Waldkirch. At Bâle the valley of the Rhine is narrow, but at a short distance below that point it begins to widen till it reaches a breadth of fifteen miles. Good roads extend along the Rhine on both sides, and bridges span the river at Bâle, Strasburg, and Mayence.

The opposing armies were thus stationed: Moreau's right wing, twenty-nine thousand strong, commanded by General Lecourbe, was in Switzerland along the Rhine from Lauffenberg to Lake Constance. Next on the left was the reserve of twenty-six thousand, commanded by Moreau in person; it occupied the intrenched camp at Bâle and extended some distance along the Rhine both above and below the city. The centre, consisting of thirty thousand soldiers, under General St. Cyr, joined the left of the reserve near Brisach, and stretched north almost to Strasburg. The left wing, nineteen thousand strong, under General Ste. Suzanne, occupied Strasburg and the bridge-head of Kehl on the opposite shore. Besides these forces, about twenty-six thousand were occupying Switzerland and the frontier fortresses of France along the Rhine as far north as Mayence.

On the Austrian side, sixteen thousand soldiers, under General Starray, were posted from Mayence to Renchen; and fifteen thousand, under General Kienmayer, were guarding the defiles of the Black Forest from Renchen to the Höllenthal. These

two corps constituted Kray's right wing. The
main body, forty thousand strong, commanded
by Kray himself, was at Villingen and Donaueschingen; and the reserve, numbering nineteen thousand, was guarding the Austrian magazines at
Stokach.   Cavalry detachments and outposts, to
the number of about five thousand, from these
several corps, were observing the Rhine and the
defiles of the Black Forest; and an Austrian
flotilla was on Lake Constance.   Beyond the lake
was Kray's left wing, numbering about twenty-five
thousand men, of whom six or seven thousand
were Tyrolese militia.   This wing was commanded
by Prince de Reuss, and extended well up into the
mountains bordering eastern Switzerland, thence
eastward into the Tyrol.

The natural base of operations for Kray's army
was the Bohemian Mountains and the Enns River,
which are about two hundred miles east of the
Black Forest.   The Austrian lines of communication to this base were over two roads: one by way
of Stokach, Memmingen, and Munich; the other
along the Danube by way of Mosskirch, Ulm, and
Ratisbon.   The temporary base of operations for
the Austrians in the Black Forest was Ulm.   At
this place, during the preceding year, the Archduke Charles had constructed an immense intrenched camp.

Knowing that it was necessary to gain a decisive
victory over the Austrians in the Black Forest be-

fore the Army of Reserve could begin its operations in Italy, the First Consul submitted a plan of
campaign which he desired Moreau to carry out.
Bonaparte proposed that Moreau should concentrate his forces on the south side of the Rhine
between Schaffhausen and Lake Constance, cross
the river in force, and attack the flank and rear of
the Austrians in the Black Forest. He calculated
that, by an attack in this direction, Moreau would
be able to defeat Kray, sever his communications,
and either capture or destroy his army.

To this plan Moreau objected. It seemed to
him a difficult operation. Cautious by nature, he
looked upon the proposed manœuvres of Bonaparte as being too bold and hazardous. He
argued that his left and centre would have to
make long flank marches in order to join his
right; and that while the movements were taking
place Kray would be given the opportunity of
concentrating his forces near Schaffhausen, where
he could oppose the passage of the French corps,
or crush them in detail as they crossed the river.

The First Consul replied that the Rhine afforded
just the kind of protection necessary to screen the
French corps during their concentration; and
that these manœuvres, if successfully executed,
would, in a short time, bring about great results.

But Moreau, who appreciated the difficulties
of forcing the passage of a large river in the face
of an active enemy, believed that the risk was too

great, and therefore refused to attempt the execution of Bonaparte's plan. Instead, he proposed the following plan. His left, under Ste. Suzanne, was to cross the Rhine at Kehl, and his centre, under St. Cyr, at Brisach. Both corps were to push forward, attack Kienmayer, and drive him into the defiles of the Black Forest. Moreau calculated that these attacks would lead Kray to believe that the French forces were massing in front of his right wing, and would cause him to re-enforce Kienmayer. Having driven the Austrians back into the Black Forest, and thus given the impression that the principal attack of the French would be made from the direction of Strasburg, Ste. Suzanne and St. Cyr were to withdraw suddenly. The former was to recross the Rhine at Kehl, ascend the river, cross again to the German side at Brisach, and take the position formerly occupied by St. Cyr; the latter was to make a flank march over the spurs and hills towards Schaffhausen by way of St. Blazien. Meanwhile Moreau with the reserve was to cross the Rhine at Bâle and march towards Schaffhausen, where, upon his arrival, his right, under Lecourbe, was to cross the river and join him. As soon as these movements were completed, Ste. Suzanne was to march towards Lake Constance by way of Friburg, Neustadt, and Loffingen. By this series of complicated manœuvres, Moreau expected to unite the bulk of his forces in the vicinity of Schaffhausen, and to march thence against the flank of Kray in the Black Forest.

Though the First Consul was anxious to have his plan adopted; though he had, in fact, already begun to collect boats in the Rhine preparatory to crossing the river near Schaffhausen, yet Moreau persisted in his own views. Nevertheless, Bonaparte hoped to convince him. With this end in view, he explained the proposed manœuvres and pointed out their advantages to General Dessoles, Moreau's chief of staff. Through this officer, who had an acute intellect and sound judgment, the First Consul hoped to change the views of Moreau himself. Though General Dessoles soon perceived that the plan of Bonaparte was superior to that of Moreau, nevertheless he advised the First Consul to allow Moreau to carry out his own ideas. "Your plan," said he to Bonaparte, "is grander, more decisive, and probably even surer; but it is not adapted to the genius of the man who is to execute it. You have a method of making war which is superior to all others; Moreau has his own, — inferior doubtless to yours, but still an excellent one. Leave him to himself; he will act well, slowly perhaps, but surely; and he will obtain as many results for you as are necessary for the success of your general combinations. If, on the contrary, you impose your ideas on him, you will disconcert him, you will wound his self-love, and obtain nothing from him by seeking to

7

obtain too much." The First Consul appreciated the wisdom of these remarks, coming from such a man, and yielded the point. " You are right," said he to General Dessoles. " Moreau is not capable of grasping and executing the plan that I have conceived. Let him follow his own course; only let him push back Marshal Kray upon Ulm and Ratisbon, and afterwards move his right wing in time upon Switzerland. The plan which he does not understand, and dares not execute, I myself will carry out on another part of the theatre of war. What he dares not attempt on the Rhine, I will accomplish on the Alps."

It being settled that Moreau should proceed against the Austrians in his own way, Bonaparte now wished to come to an understanding with him by which a corps of twenty or twenty-five thousand men should, at the proper time, be detached from the Army of the Rhine, and be sent across Switzerland to unite in Italy with the Army of Reserve. But Moreau did not enter heartily into any of the plans proposed by the First Consul. In fact, both he and Bonaparte seemed to distrust each other. Whether from jealousy, or from honest convictions, Moreau opposed the plans of Bonaparte. Moreover, he had declared that he would not serve under the First Consul, should the latter unite the Army of Reserve with the Army of the Rhine. Naturally this opposition created in the mind of Bonaparte a doubt of Moreau's good faith.

He feared that, at the critical moment, the commander of the Army of the Rhine might fail to send a corps into Italy. He was well aware that the commander of an army is always reluctant to weaken his forces after operations have begun; and he knew that circumstances might arise which would seem to justify Moreau in refusing to obey the orders of his superior. He therefore insisted that Moreau should sign a stipulation whereby he promised that, after pushing Kray back from Lake Constance, he would detach Lecourbe with twenty or twenty-five thousand men, and order him into Italy. This agreement was signed at Bâle by Moreau and General Berthier, the latter representing the First Consul.

Nearly a month had passed since the arrangements between Bonaparte and Moreau had been completed. It was now the latter part of April, yet Moreau had made no movement to cross the Rhine and attack Kray. Naturally cautious and slow, he had postponed his advance from day to day, in order, if possible, to supply his army with everything necessary to increase its fighting power. He was short of cavalry and artillery horses, and had little or no camp equipage, and no intrenching tools. But at this time it was impossible for him to obtain everything he needed. Already Bonaparte had sent to the Army of the Rhine all the spare material of war that he could collect in France. Now he was anxious to have Moreau

advance. Masséna was hard pressed at Genoa,
and Bonaparte desired to march into Italy in
order to relieve him. But to cross the Alps and
throw himself upon the rear of Melas, while Kray
remained undefeated in the Black Forest, was too
hazardous an undertaking. Much therefore depended upon the early advance of Moreau. Repeatedly Bonaparte urged him to press forward,
and finally sent him a positive order to cross the
Rhine and attack Kray.

On the 25th of April Moreau began his movement. Ste. Suzanne crossed the Rhine at Kehl,
ascended the Kinzig valley, and pushed Kienmayer's outposts back into the Black Forest. At
the same time St. Cyr crossed at Brisach; one
division of his corps then advanced towards the
Kinzig valley, while the other divisions forced
back the Austrians at Friburg, and occupied the
entrance to the Höllenthal.

On the next day Kray at Donaueschingen heard
of these movements. Having received word that
a part of his right wing had been attacked by
forty thousand men, he was led to believe that
Moreau intended to force his way through the
Black Forest by way of the Kinzig valley. He
therefore sent seven thousand Austrians from
Villingen to re-enforce Kienmayer, and to replace
these troops withdrew seven thousand men from
his reserve at Stokach. At the same time he
ordered his extreme right, under Starray, to move

towards the main army into the valley of the Murg.

On the 27th of April Ste. Suzanne withdrew his corps from its advanced position preparatory to recrossing the Rhine at Kehl. St. Cyr, having directed his artillery and trains to follow the river road on the right bank towards Schaffhausen, led his infantry across the hills towards St. Blazien. Moreau crossed the Rhine at Bâle with the reserve; one of his divisions, commanded by General Richepanse, then ascended the Weiss River, so as to join the right of St. Cyr's corps; the other two, commanded by Moreau in person, marched up the Rhine towards Schaffhausen.

On the following day Ste. Suzanne recrossed at Kehl, and proceeded up the left bank of the Rhine towards Brisach. St. Cyr, having united a part of his forces with Richepanse's division, occupied St. Blazien. Moreau himself forced a passage across the Alle River, and drove back an Austrian brigade there, which retreated towards Bonndorf.

On the 30th of April Ste. Suzanne, having arrived at Brisach, again crossed the Rhine to the German side, and took up the position at Friburg, at the entrance to the Höllenthal, recently occupied by St. Cyr's troops. St. Cyr remained in the vicinity of St. Blazien. Moreau advanced upon the Wutach River, and Lecourbe concentrated his corps on the south bank of the Rhine near Schaff-

hausen, preparatory to crossing the river at that
point.

Thus the French corps continued to push forward. On the 1st of May Moreau reached Schaffhausen, where he was joined by Lecourbe's corps,
part of which crossed the river in boats, and the
remainder over a bridge temporarily constructed
for the purpose. St. Cyr reached Stuhlingen, and
Ste. Suzanne, having driven back the Austrian
brigade occupying the Höllenthal, arrived at
Neustadt.

During these movements the Austrian outposts
along the Rhine fell back before Moreau to
Stuhlingen, and, upon St. Cyr's arrival at that
place, retreated upon Zollhaus. Meanwhile Kray
had directed part of his own immediate command
upon Loffingen and Zollhaus. Kienmayer, with
the greater part of his forces, still remained in the
valley of the Kinzig, and Starray in the valley of
the Murg.

Thus the first part of Moreau's plan was successfully executed. As yet he had met with no
reverse. His forces had driven before them the
Austrian outposts and advance brigades, till now
three of his corps, numbering eighty-five thousand
men, were within supporting distance of one
another on the north side of the Rhine near Schaffhausen. From this favorable position he could
march at once against Kray in the Black Forest,
and outnumber him almost two to one; for Kray

could not expect immediate aid from his left wing, which was beyond Lake Constance on the borders of eastern Switzerland and in the Tyrol, or from his right wing, which was far away in the valleys of the Kinzig and the Murg.

Kray now began to appreciate the insecurity of his position. He perceived that his reserve and immense magazines at Stokach were in danger. Should Moreau capture this place and push rapidly forward towards Ulm, he would sever the Austrian communications, and thus place Kray in a position where a defeat would ruin his army. In order to prevent, if possible, such a result, Kray decided to unite his forces at Stokach, and there give battle to Moreau. With this end in view, Kray caused the following movements to be made. On the 2d of May the Austrian brigade that had been driven from Neustadt by the advance of Ste. Suzanne, moved to Bonndorf; the Austrians at Bonndorf marched to Zollhaus; and those at Zollhaus, to Geisingen, where Kray had collected the Austrian troops under his immediate command. On the 3d of May his columns advanced towards Stokach over the Geisingen-Engen road.

Meanwhile Moreau was not idle. On the 3d of May he moved on Engen with the reserve; St. Cyr on Zollhaus; and Lecourbe, having directed two brigades to ascend the Aach River, in order to connect with the right of the reserve, marched on Stokach with about twenty thousand men, attacked and defeated the twelve thousand Austrians there, captured the immense magazines, and forced the Austrians back towards Ulm by way of Mosskirch and by way of Memmingen. But after this victory Lecourbe, not receiving any orders from Moreau to push forward and seize Mosskirch, remained in the vicinity of Stokach, awaiting the result of the operations of Moreau at Engen.

Meanwhile Kray, on his way to Stokach, had reached Engen before the arrival of Moreau. In this position his troops, numbering about forty-five thousand men, faced south with their left at Engen and their right extended towards Zollhaus. Moreau soon arrived with the reserve. His forces, counting the two brigades on his right detached from Lecourbe's corps, numbered about forty thousand men. At once Moreau began the battle. Fiercely and desperately the French and Austrians fought for several hours, but neither gained a decided advantage. Finally, late in the day, St. Cyr, who had received orders from Moreau to hurry forward from Zollhaus, arrived and began an attack upon the right of the Austrians, which caused them to give way. But this attack was made too late to produce any decisive result. The Austrians, though forced at last to yield, were not crushed; in fact, Engen was little more than a drawn battle. But, during the night, Kray, having learned of the capture of Stokach, began to fear

that Lecourbe would push forward, seize Mosskirch, and sever his communications with Ulm.
He therefore decided to retreat. Leaving a rear
guard to hold Moreau in check, he directed his
forces upon Tuttlingen, Liptengen, and Mosskirch. At the battle of Engen each side lost in
killed, wounded, and captured, about seven thousand men.

Kray now determined to unite as many of his
troops as possible at Mosskirch, and there to make
a stand against the French, who were pushing
eagerly forward towards Ulm. Already he had
sent word to General Starray and General Kienmayer to descend the left bank of the Danube,
and join him at the earliest possible moment.

On the 4th of May Moreau directed his own
corps and that of Lecourbe on Mosskirch; St.
Cyr arrived at Geisingen; and Ste. Suzanne, who
had been forcing his way through the Black
Forest, was at Donaueschingen.

On the following day Kray, having been joined
by the remnants of his reserve, beaten at Stokach,
took position at Mosskirch with forty thousand
men. His right was at Tuttlingen, about twelve
miles distant; but Kienmayer and Starray were
beyond supporting distance on the north side of
the Danube. On this day Moreau attacked Kray
with fifty thousand men, and, after hard fighting,
succeeded in forcing the Austrians back towards
Sigmaringen. But Kray did not retire far. Being

anxious for the safety of the Austrian troops at Tuttlingen, he halted, formed line of battle, and with the right of his line strongly re-enforced, attacked the French and drove them from the Tuttlingen-Mosskirch road. This success opened his communications with the Austrians at Tuttlingen, and enabled them to join him. Being thus re-enforced, he again attacked the left flank of Moreau, and attempted to seize the Stokach-Mosskirch road. But in his attempt to outflank the French, he was in turn outflanked by them, and was again compelled to retire.

In the battle of Mosskirch the Austrians lost in killed, wounded, and prisoners, about five thousand men; the French, about three thousand. In this battle both sides fought fiercely, but neither gained a decided success. Nevertheless, Kray saw the necessity of retreating; for St. Cyr, who had taken no part in the battle, was now about to join Moreau; and Ste. Suzanne was pushing rapidly forward towards Mosskirch by way of Tuttlingen. In other words, Kray, with less than fifty thousand men, could not expect to hold his own in a second battle at Mosskirch against the united French corps.

Kray crossed the Danube at Sigmaringen, and, being joined by the two corps of his right wing, retired towards Ulm by way of Rietlingen and Biberach. He was followed by Moreau. Lecourbe marched by way of Memmingen, St. Cyr by way of

Biberach, and Ste. Suzanne descended the Danube
towards Ulm. At Biberach Kray attempted to
make a stand, in order to save the Austrian magazines there, but was defeated with considerable
loss. Lecourbe also defeated an Austrian garrison occupying Memmingen, and captured the
place.

On the 11th of May Kray continued his retreat
on Ulm, which, through the foresight of the Archduke Charles in the preceding year, had been
converted into a strongly intrenched camp. At
Ulm Kray sought and found safety for his army.
Here he collected the shattered remains of his
defeated forces, and for several weeks made a successful stand against Moreau. Here, eyeing each
other with suspicion, these two armies remained
for a time, each ready to take advantage of any
false movement of the other, while more stirring
operations and greater deeds were happening in
the valley of the Po.

It is difficult to estimate accurately the losses
sustained by the contending armies in these operations. Probably the loss of the Austrians was
about twenty thousand men; that of the French,
about fifteen thousand. At the opening of hostilities, Kray's forces, not counting the left wing
under the Prince de Reuss, since it took no part
in the active operations, numbered ninety-five
thousand men. At Ulm Kray had seventy-five
thousand. On the other hand, Moreau had crossed

the Rhine with one hundred and four thousand soldiers, and had reached Ulm with nearly ninety thousand; but he was about to send fifteen thousand men into Italy, which would leave the opposing armies about equal in numbers.

The time had arrived for the commander of the Army of the Rhine to carry out the agreement entered into between himself and the First Consul. In fact, since the battle of Engen, Bonaparte had awaited anxiously for Moreau to start the promised re-enforcements towards Italy. Fearing that Moreau might still delay in the matter, the First Consul had sent Carnot, the French minister of war, to Moreau's headquarters, in order to make the necessary arrangements, and to insist that the troops should be detached and ordered forward at the earliest possible moment.

Moreau did not comply fully with the agreement entered into with the First Consul, but on the 11th and 12th of May he selected fifteen thousand men from the different French corps, united these troops into a single corps and ordered it to proceed into Italy.

Though Moreau had not succeeded in severing the communications of Kray, and in capturing or destroying his army, he had been generally successful in his manœuvres; he had pushed the Austrians back from Lake Constance, defeated them at Stokach and Engen, forced them to retreat after the battle of Mosskirch, and compelled them to seek security in the intrenched camp of Ulm. Though he had retained General Lecourbe and his corps in the valley of the Danube, and had failed to send into Italy the full number agreed upon in the stipulation with the First Consul, nevertheless, he had weakened his army by fifteen thousand men, and, by so doing, had given Bonaparte the opportunity of bringing to a successful issue one of the most striking and dramatic campaigns of his career.

COMMENTS.

In order to understand clearly the strategical problems presented by these operations, it is necessary to keep in mind the positions of the French and Austrian forces, and the topography of the country in which these manœuvres and battles took place.

Picture to yourself the French forces occupying Switzerland and France on the left bank of the Rhine as far north as Strasburg; and on the opposite side of the river, the long line of the Austrians, their left on the borders of eastern Switzerland and in the Tyrol, their right extending far to the north, even to Mayence, and their centre, forming the main part of the Austrian army, occupying the Black Forest with advanced brigades and outposts pushed forward almost to the banks of the Rhine. Picture to yourself the triangular mountain system of the Black Forest, lying in the angle of the Rhine between Lake Constance and Strasburg, like a huge bastion, its south and west sides steep and rugged, and its hills and mountains covered with a dark forest of pines and firs. Picture to yourself the fifteen thousand Austrians, under Kienmayer, along the rugged west face of this mountain group; the forty thousand, under the immediate command of Marshal Kray, lying on the eastern slope of this great barrier of mountains and hills; the reserve of nineteen thousand at Stokach on the direct road between Schaffhausen and Ulm, and but a day's march from the French in Switzerland; the magazines at Stokach, Engen, Mosskirch, and Biberach, upon which Kray depended for his supplies; and the immense intrenched camp at Ulm, which, lying in his rear upon the Danube, was the temporary base of the Austrians in the Black Forest.

By occupying all the valleys, roads, and prominent points in the theatre of operations, the Austrians expected to hold military possession of the country. Their system of war was to form a chain of posts — a cordon — along the line to be occupied; and by this means they expected to prevent the advance of the enemy. Thus the Austrian army was scattered over a great extent of country from the Tyrol to Lake Constance, thence through the Black Forest to the Main

River. Their line was more than three hundred miles in extent.

Kray had extended his right wing as far north as Mayence, in order to protect the troops in the Black Forest from a French attack on that side. Since Moreau held the line of the Rhine, possibly he might attempt to cross at Mayence, thence, using the Main River to screen his movements, might march to Wurtzburg, and from that point march south on Ulm. By such a manœuvre, he could sever Kray's communications, take the Austrians in rear in the Black Forest, and compel them to fight with their face towards Vienna, in order to recover their communications. But, in order to protect himself on this side, Kray had extended Starray's corps too far north; it consisted of but sixteen thousand soldiers, and was so scattered from Mayence to Renchen, a distance of one hundred miles, that it was weak at all points. Moreover, it was so far distant from the main Austrian forces in the Black Forest that it could neither readily aid them in case they should be attacked in force, nor be readily aided by them should Moreau attempt to make a flank movement against the Austrian right.

But a greater fault in the situation of the Austrian army was due to the fact that the Aulic Council had given orders that Kray's left wing, under the Prince de Reuss, should remain on the borders of eastern Switzerland and in the Tyrol.

This wing could not, therefore, re-enforce Kray in the Black Forest. With his left thus paralyzed by the action of the Aulic Council, Kray found himself hampered throughout the campaign.

Kray committed another error in collecting immense magazines at Stokach; for this place, being but a day's march from the French forces in Switzerland, was not only the most vulnerable but also the most important point occupied by the Austrians. Lying in a gap between Lake Constance and the mountains of Switzerland on one side, and the Black Forest on the other, and being on the direct road from Schaffhausen to Ulm, it was, so to speak, the vital point of the long Austrian line. Along this route the French would be most likely to advance into Germany; for they could ascend the Rhine by the river roads, thence proceed to Stokach, and thus avoid the great natural barrier of the Black Forest. Moreover, by adopting this plan there were great strategical advantages to be gained.

First: Should the French capture Stokach, they would permanently separate the Austrian left from the centre and right. Thus they would divide the forces of the Austrians, and might thereafter be able to defeat them in detail.

Second: Should the French capture Stokach, they would be in a favorable position to march north against the Austrians and sever their communications with Ulm. In this position, the French, if defeated, could fall back to Schaffhausen, and recross the river there with little or no danger of losing their communications ; but the Austrians, being obliged to form their line of battle parallel, or nearly so, to the roads leading to their base, would, if defeated, be thrown back into the Black Forest, where doubtless they would be captured or destroyed. In short, the success of the French at Stokach would enable them to carry out two great principles of war: not only would they divide the forces of their enemy, and thus eventually be able to defeat them in detail; but they would gain a position where they could threaten the communications of Kray in the Black Forest without exposing their own to his attacks.

In the angle of the Rhine between Lake Constance and Strasburg, Kray had but eighty thousand soldiers. Upon this force he had to rely in order to repel any attack which the French might make in the Black Forest; for his extreme right, under Starray, and his left, under Prince de Reuss, were too far away to support his centre before the French could unite to attack it. Bearing in mind that the French crossed the Rhine with one hundred and four thousand soldiers, we perceive that the opportunity was offered Moreau of bringing superior numbers against Kray. In other words, should both opposing commanders succeed in uniting all their available forces upon a battle-field in the Black Forest, Moreau would outnumber

Kray in about the proportion of four to three. As the first principle of war is to be stronger than the enemy at the vital point, it is always of the greatest importance that no plan of campaign be adopted, which shall, at the very start, allow the enemy to bring superior numbers on the battle-field.

In withdrawing seven thousand men from Stokach to replace the seven thousand sent from Villingen to re-enforce Kienmayer, Kray committed another error. In fact, at the outset of the campaign he weakened the garrison of the most important point of the whole Austrian line, by sending away more than one third of the troops there. Thus, unconsciously, he played into the hands of his adversary; for at the very time that these troops were leaving Stokach, Moreau was so regulating his manœuvres as to make in the near future his first great effort against Kray at or near that place.

Had the left wing of the Austrian army not been ordered to remain along the eastern borders of Switzerland, it would seem that it might have marched north along the east side of Lake Constance, and have struck the flank and rear of the French as they proceeded from Stokach towards Ulm. Doubtless such a manœuvre would have produced great results; but it must be remembered that the French, still in Switzerland, might then have crossed the Rhine above Lake Constance, and have attacked the flank and rear of the Austrian left wing.

Says General Hamley: —

" In former years the base of the Republican armies
operating in Germany had been some part of the straight
course of the Rhine, from its corner at Bâle to Dussel-
dorf. Their eminent adversary, the Archduke Charles,
says that the strong line of the Rhine, and the line of
French fortresses behind it, can only be assailed by the
Austrians in circumstances unusually favorable. All that
can be done is to approach and choose a position where
the plans of the enemy may be defeated, his advance
stopped, and the country behind covered.

" The armies on the Rhine had hitherto been on parallel fronts; the Austrians generally on the defensive, since
the exceptionally favorable circumstances which could
alone enable them to assume the offensive by passing the
Rhine had not existed. The French, breaking out at
one or the other of the bridge-heads which they possessed
on the river, would try to press forward into Germany;
the Austrians, drawing together on the threatened points,
would oppose them : and the result was that, in 1800,
the river still formed the frontier line between them.

" But in 1800 a new condition had entered into the
problem of a campaign on the Rhine. The French had
occupied Switzerland, an act which entailed military
results such as few generals of that time had the foresight to
appreciate. One was to carry the French base onward
from Bâle, round the angle to Schaffhausen. Thus that
base, originally straight, was now rectangular, and enclosed within it a part of the theatre of war."

Herein is to be found in part the explanation
of Kray's faulty arrangement of his forces. Had

Switzerland been neutral territory, his reserve and magazines at Stokach would not have been within striking distance of the French. Had Switzerland been neutral territory, the French could not have made a flank movement against his forces in the Black Forest, and thus have been given the opportunity of severing his communications with Ulm. In fact, the possession of Switzerland gave many advantages to Moreau, and enabled him to force the Austrians back to Ulm, notwithstanding the fact that he committed many errors and gained no great victory.

It will now be apparent that Kray had taken up a position too far to the front; and that, by so doing, he had allowed the French to take advantage of the angular base of operations formed by northern Switzerland and eastern France. "Although Kray showed himself superior to Moreau," says Colonel Macdougall, "his faults were serious. He disseminated his army along the line of the Rhine in too forward a position, since his rear was exposed to attack by a French force operating from Schaffhausen. He established his magazines at Stokach, Engen, and Mosskirch, close to a part of the French base. If Switzerland had been friendly or neutral, his magazines in those places would have been well placed, since they would in that case have been covered by the defiles of the Black Forest; as it was, they were quite at the advanced posts."

Moreau's plan of campaign did not differ greatly from that of Bonaparte. In fact, both he and the First Consul aimed to concentrate the French in force between Schaffhausen and Lake Constance. In order to effect the concentration, however, Moreau purposed to cross the Rhine at four points, then by a series of complicated manœuvres to unite the bulk of his forces in the vicinity of Schaffhausen. On the other hand, Bonaparte's plan was to assemble the French corps on the south side of the Rhine opposite Schaffhausen, to cross the river in force near that place, and thence proceed against Kray. In an able and interesting discussion of these two plans, General Hamley says: —

"The plans of campaign of Napoleon and of Moreau had this in common, that both aimed at the communications of the Austrians by an advance from the extreme point of the angular base ; but in the mode of effecting the common object they differed materially, and the difference was the result of the individual characters of the projectors. When Napoleon's glance was once fixed on the point where decisive success lay, the obstacles in his way lost, in his mind, much of their importance, and were viewed merely as difficult steps to his object. Hence, though he neglected no provision nor precaution which prudence and experience could suggest for overcoming them, yet he never allowed them to assume an importance sufficient to deprive his plan of campaign of its fullest significance. Disregarding, therefore, the fact that he must throw his army entire at one point across a great river which was observed by the enemy, he looked only to the great results that must flow from the advance of that army, concentrated, upon the vital point of an enemy whose forces would still be in greater or less degree dispersed.

"Moreau, cautious and forecasting by nature, saw in his mind's eye the Austrian army assembled opposite Schaffhausen to oppose his passage, — baffling the whole plan. All his precautions, therefore, were framed to obviate the danger of crossing in the face of the enemy. Only one corps was to cross at Schaffhausen, — another, the reserve, was to cross at Bâle to cover the passage; this entailed the movement of a third through the mountains to cover the long flank march of the reserve along the river; and a fourth was to make a false attack in order to detain the Austrian troops in the defiles as long as possible, and prevent them from re-enforcing the left.

"It is probable that Napoleon's plan would have miscarried in the hands of Moreau; but looking at other achievements of Bonaparte, — his descent on the Austrian rear in Italy a few weeks later, — his decisive march to the Danube in 1805 on the other side of the present theatre, — it is not to be denied that, executed by himself, the design might have fulfilled all his expectations."

It is certainly an interesting fact that, notwithstanding the objections of Bonaparte to Moreau's plan, nevertheless the commander of the Army of the Rhine succeeded in assembling the bulk of his forces in the vicinity of Schaffhausen. In his own way he executed the manœuvres which, even to

Bonaparte, seemed fraught with danger. As a matter of fact, the assembling of the French corps in this position was the most critical part of the whole campaign; and it mattered not whether the concentration was made by marching on the German side of the Rhine, or by marching on the Swiss side; in either case, skill and generalship were required to carry out successfully these manœuvres. It will now be interesting to compare the plans of these two soldiers.

The line of the Rhine divided the opposing armies. At the outset the French corps crossed the river at Strasburg, Brisach, Bâle, and Schaffhausen. Moreau then attempted to unite these corps before proceeding to attack Kray in force. It is always a dangerous operation to attempt a concentration upon some designated place within the enemy's lines; for, as a rule, the enemy can mass his forces there more rapidly than can the commander of an invading army. In fact, many a campaign has failed because the commanding general has attempted to unite his scattered forces at some point within the territory held by the enemy. By so doing, he gives the enemy a chance to assemble his forces between the separated columns of the attacking army, and to bring superior numbers against each column in succession. Thus, when Moreau crossed the Rhine at Strasburg, Brisach, Bâle, and Schaffhausen, he gave Kray the opportunity of defeating in detail the several

French corps so widely separated from one another. Though the topography of the country was such that it did not allow Kray to concentrate his forces and throw them readily upon the separated French corps in succession, yet, had he foreseen the design of his adversary, undoubtedly he could have massed his forces between Schaffhausen and Bâle, along the Wutach, and have thus intervened between Lecourbe's corps and that of Moreau. By such a manœuvre, he would have stood a good chance of crushing both Moreau and St. Cyr, before they could have been re-enforced by either Ste. Suzanne or Lecourbe.

Again: Moreau's plan necessitated that his own corps and that of St. Cyr should make long flank marches on the German side of the river. In making these marches, the French corps necessarily exposed their own flanks to the attacks of the enemy. In fact, Kray might have issued in force from the Black Forest, and have attacked both Moreau and St. Cyr with great chances of success. Had he done so, doubtless these two French corps would have been destroyed; for they would have found themselves enclosed between a victorious enemy on one side and an impassable river on the other. Even when protected by a river, or other great natural obstacle, a flank march, in the vicinity of an active enemy, is often a difficult manœuvre; but when undertaken in an enemy's country, between an unfordable river on one side, and an active enemy on the other, it then becomes an extremely delicate and dangerous operation.

It will also be noticed that though St. Cyr, in his march across the hills and mountains from Friburg to St. Blazien, and thence to Stuhlingen, flanked and protected the reserve in its march from Bâle to Schaffhausen, yet he was obliged to send his artillery by the river road. Had he, therefore, been attacked in force during this movement, he would have been compelled to fight without his artillery. Thus the fighting power of his corps would have been diminished; and his efforts would have been directed towards the protection of his cannon, which, under ordinary circumstances, should have strengthened, instead of weakened, him.

In commenting on these operations of Moreau, General Hamley says: —

"The false attacks of Ste. Suzanne and St. Cyr had the effect not only of detaining Kienmayer's sixteen thousand men in the defiles, but of causing Kray to move thither six or seven thousand additional troops. But they had no influence in detaining Starray, who was already so distant on the right that it would be impossible for him in any case to join Kray in time for the first operations. We find, then, that at first forty-nine thousand French were employed in detaining less than half their number; and when St. Cyr had joined the reserve, still Ste. Suzanne did not probably neutralise a greater number of the enemy than his own corps. The detached operations of Ste. Suzanne appear, therefore, dangerous and fruitless."

Consider now the plan of Bonaparte. It is evident that the line of the Rhine from Strasburg to Lake Constance would have screened the French corps during their concentration. Since this unfordable river and the bridges crossing it were in possession of the French, there was little probability that the French corps would have been attacked in flank during their march up the Rhine to Schaffhausen. In fact, the Rhine and the mountains of the Black Forest, behind which the greater part of the Austrians lay, would have formed such a complete screen to the operations of Bonaparte that it is not improbable to suppose that the proposed French concentration, preparatory to crossing the river, might have been completed before Kray discovered what was in progress. Moreover, since this plan involved no complicated manœuvres, it could have been carried out more quickly than the plan of Moreau. Thus time would have been saved; and *time* was then of the greatest importance to Bonaparte, inasmuch as Masséna was in desperate straits at Genoa.

The same reason makes it probable that the passage of the river at Schaffhausen, the most difficult problem of Bonaparte's plan of campaign, might have been accomplished before Kray learned the designs of his adversary. Another fact confirms this view. It will be remembered that, after Moreau crossed the Rhine with his four corps, twenty-six thousand French soldiers still remained in Switzerland and in the French fortresses along the Rhine. Inasmuch as a part of this force was occupying Strasburg, it is quite probable that, had Bonaparte's plan been adopted, a division of four or five thousand men would have issued from the bridge-head opposite this place, and have attacked the Austrians on the west side of the Black Forest. Such an attack would probably have deceived Kray, and have left him in doubt as to where the French intended to cross the river in force; it would probably have caused him to leave Kienmayer's corps in its position, and have prevented him from uniting a sufficient force in the vicinity of Schaffhausen to oppose the passage of the French.

It will be remembered that Bonaparte had already made some preparations for crossing the Rhine near Schaffhausen; he had secretly collected a number of boats on the river between Bâle and Lake Constance. These boats were to be used for the crossing of the advance divisions. The purpose also was to throw two or three bridges across the river; the material for which could have been collected and prepared by Lecourbe's corps while the remaining corps were ascending the Rhine.

It will also be noticed that the point selected by Bonaparte for the crossing was a favorable one. During the passage Lake Constance would have protected the right flank of the French corps from an Austrian attack, and would have continued to protect them as they marched towards Stokach.

Though the crossing of a large river in the face of an active enemy is a difficult operation, yet it is generally successful, because great pains is nearly always taken to deceive the enemy, and because great preparations are nearly always made to insure the success of the operation. " If," says Jomini, " we take into consideration the great care and precautions that are requisite, the immense amount of materials employed in such an operation, the concurrence of circumstances necessary to secure success, and the difficulties which may be occasioned by the slightest derangement on the part of the enemy, it is really surprising that an operation of this kind ever succeeds. Nevertheless, wonderful as it may seem, the most difficult military enterprises are commonly the most successful, from the simple fact that greater care and precautions are employed in their execution."

From the foregoing it is apparent that the manœuvres of Moreau were not wisely planned. In appearance only they seemed to be less hazardous than those of Bonaparte. After magnifying the difficulties of crossing the Rhine with the four French corps at Schaffhausen, Moreau adopted a course which was much more complicated, which required a longer time to execute, which involved several strategical errors, and which, as will be shown later, did not allow Moreau to take all the advantages of the angular base of operations due to his possession of Switzerland. Though these manœuvres were successful, it is not because they were wisely planned, but because there was little or no opposition to their execution. They were successful because Kray, not appreciating the situation, failed to profit by the mistakes of his adversary.

It will now be of interest to examine into the operations of Moreau after he had united the bulk of his forces in the vicinity of Schaffhausen.

On the 1st of May the four French corps were thus stationed: Moreau's and Lecourbe's at Schaffhausen, St. Cyr's at Stuhlingen, and Ste. Suzanne's at Neustadt. From these positions the French advanced to attack Kray. Lecourbe with twenty thousand men marched on Stokach to capture that place, and to drive back the Austrian reserve of twelve thousand there; Moreau moved on Engen with forty thousand men and there encountered Kray with forty-five thousand; St. Cyr directed his corps on Zollhaus; and Ste. Suzanne remained in the vicinity of Neustadt. In front of St. Cyr and Ste. Suzanne there were a few thousand Austrian troops more or less scattered. Kienmayer's corps yet remained along the western edge of the Black Forest, and Starray's corps was still farther away toward the north.

Though Moreau had assembled three of his corps, numbering eighty-five thousand men, in such positions that they could easily have concentrated upon a single battle-field, and have outnumbered Kray almost two to one; yet, at the battle of Engen, he was outnumbered by his adversary. St. Cyr's corps was so far away to the left that it had scarcely any effect in deciding the battle. Evidently this corps should have been so directed that it could have re-enforced the right of Moreau or the left of Lecourbe. Had this been done, the battle of Engen would have been a great victory. Then Moreau could have hurled the Austrians back into the Black Forest, and have severed their communications with Ulm. In short, Moreau should have advanced with his right, instead of his left, strongly re-enforced. In order to reap the full advantages of the flank position which he occupied, every effort should have been made so to defeat the Austrians as to get possession of their communications. Moreau failed to appreciate this fact. His faulty movements enabled Kray, after the battle of Engen, to fall back to Mosskirch; and, by so doing, to retain possession of the road to Ulm.

It is evident, too, that Lecourbe's corps, after its victory at Stokach, should have pushed forward and seized Mosskirch and the roads leading to Ulm; but it failed to do so, because Moreau did not send Lecourbe the necessary orders. After the capture of the most important place occupied by the Austrians, this corps remained inactive for a time, knowing not what to do or where to march.

Why did Moreau fail to send the necessary orders to Lecourbe? Why did he thus scatter his three corps? Why was St. Cyr directed upon Zollhaus, instead of upon Engen or Stokach? These are interesting questions, and their answers will perhaps enable us to form a correct estimate of the military ability of Moreau.

In retaining the direct command of a corps, Moreau committed a fault. He should have appointed a corps commander of the reserve, and have left himself free to give greater attention to the movements of his entire army. As it was he was wrapped up in what his own corps was doing. As long as the soldiers directly under him were victorious, he seemed to be satisfied. Perhaps, from this cause, or from the fact that he failed to appreciate the strategical situation, the significance and importance of Lecourbe's victory at Stokach did not impress itself upon him. Thus no orders were given for Lecourbe's corps to hasten forward and seize Mosskirch. Moreau's military horizon was limited; his glance failed to sweep the whole theatre of operations.

That his corps were scattered was due in great measure to the plan of campaign that he had adopted. In carrying out this plan, Ste. Suzanne had marched through the Höllenthal, and was near Neustadt when the French attacked the Aus-

trians at Engen and Stokach. Moreau realized
that Stokach and Engen were the important points
of the Austrian line; yet, rather than leave Ste.
Suzanne's corps isolated at Neustadt, where possibly it might be crushed by overwhelming numbers, he directed St. Cyr's corps on Zollhaus, so
that it might, if necessary, re-enforce Ste. Suzanne.
Thus it was that his four corps were spread out
from Stokach to Neustadt; and that St. Cyr's
corps was directed upon the left instead of upon
the right of Moreau. Thus it was that his plan
prevented him from taking full advantage of the
angular base which the possession of Switzerland
gave to the French.

But, notwithstanding the fact that Ste. Suzanne's
corps was at Neustadt, St. Cyr's corps should not
have been directed upon Zollhaus. Now, it might
seem to us, as it undoubtedly seemed to Moreau,
that, had St. Cyr's corps marched directly to the
support of the French at Engen or Stokach, Ste.
Suzanne's corps would have been left in an isolated and dangerous position where it could have
been captured or destroyed. But such was not
the case; indeed, there were several reasons why
Kray would not have attempted to concentrate
against Ste. Suzanne.

First: The movement of the French right on
Stokach and Engen threatened the communications of Kray, without in the least exposing the
communications of Moreau to an Austrian attack.

In accordance with a maxim of war, proved by experience, Kray would therefore have abandoned any intended attack upon Ste. Suzanne, in order to fight for the preservation of his own communications. "The commander," says Hamley, "who finds himself on his enemy's rear, while his own is still beyond the adversary's reach, may cast aside all anxiety for his own communications, and call up every detachment to the decisive point, certain that the enemy will abandon his own designs, in order, if possible, to retrieve his position." Had Moreau appreciated this fact, he could have safely united three of his corps near Stokach, and have overwhelmed the Austrians with superior numbers.

Second: Though Ste. Suzanne seemed to be in a dangerous position, he was not so in reality. In fact, had Kray attacked Ste. Suzanne in force near Neustadt, he would have given the French at Engen and Stokach an immense advantage; for the farther he proceeded into the Black Forest towards France, the more easily could the French sever his communications and destroy or capture his army.

Third: Instead, therefore, of Moreau's being fearful lest the Austrians should concentrate against Ste. Suzanne, he should rather have hoped to see them carry out this movement. But, in either case, he should have strongly re-enforced his right by every means in his power.

After the battle of Engen, Moreau continued to commit errors. At Mosskirch he attacked the Austrians with but fifty thousand men. At the beginning of the battle Kray had but forty thousand men, yet before it ended he was strongly reenforced. During the battle St. Cyr's corps was near Geisingen and Ste. Suzanne's at Donaueschingen. Thus, for the second time, Moreau fought the Austrians with two of his corps absent. Moreover, they were far away on his left flank, when they should have been near him, or on his right flank, where they would have been able to overwhelm Kray, and sever his communications with Ulm. Had Moreau re-enforced strongly his right, and attacked Kray at Mosskirch with his four corps, or even with three of them, who can doubt what the result would have been? Undoubtedly he would have destroyed the Austrians between his army and the Danube, and could then have rapidly crossed the river and have intercepted the corps of Kienmayer and Starray. In truth, Moreau's faults allowed Kray to escape, when he should have been destroyed. They allowed him to seek safety in Ulm, where for several weeks he was able to make a successful stand.

This part of Moreau's campaign, from the time he left Schaffhausen till he arrived at Ulm, was a series of errors. Though in a measure successful in his operations, he was outgeneralled by Kray.

In this campaign every opportunity was offered
Moreau to win a great name, but he did not pos-
sess the necessary military ability. He was in command of the largest and best equipped army of
France; instead of gaining merely two or three in-
decisive victories and forcing Kray back to Ulm, he
should have united his forces, crushed his enemy,
severed Kray's communications, and captured his
army; and then should have marched on Vienna
and compelled the Austrian Emperor to sue for
peace. But such fame was not for him. It was reserved for that greater genius, who, beyond the
Alps, on the plains of Italy, should, with inferior
forces, do greater deeds and accomplish far greater
results. It was reserved for him who, daring to follow in the footsteps of the great Carthaginian, was
destined to startle the world by the splendor of
his achievements.

If there was one distinguishing peculiarity in
Napoleon's system of war, it was that of so manœuvring as to divide the forces of his enemy and
then to defeat them in detail. In the early part
of his career he was fortunate in being opposed
to the Austrians, whose system of scattering their
troops enabled him to defeat separately the fragments of their armies. He believed in concentrating his troops. He was, in fact, the greatest
exemplar of concentration that the world has ever
known. His plan was to mass his forces against

some vital point of the enemy, and to attack him on one line, and in such a direction as to place him at a disadvantage. If the enemy's line was too much extended, he struck at the centre and broke through it, then attacked and defeated in detail the separated parts. If the enemy advanced to attack with his army separated into parts by impassable obstacles, Napoleon manœuvred so as to crush in succession these isolated parts before they could unite. In this way, by fighting a part of the enemy's army at one time, he was nearly always stronger than the enemy on the battle-field. With him this was the important point. His rapid marches, his strategical manœuvres, his combinations, had nearly always this object in view. He believed that success in battle depended principally on numbers. " God," said he, " is on the side of the heaviest battalions."

But notwithstanding the fact that this was the distinguishing peculiarity of Napoleon's system of war, yet he did not always follow this system. Several times in his career he won a great victory by making a flank movement against his enemy. Such a movement was made at Marengo, at Ulm, and at Jena.

Between these two methods of attack there is, as a rule, this difference. By striking at the centre of the enemy's line, his army can be separated into two parts, and then be defeated in detail. In this case the aim is so to manœuvre as to outnumber the enemy on the battle-field. But by striking at the flank, the enemy is often given the opportunity of concentrating his forces. Even if one flank is defeated, it can fall back upon the other, and perhaps even then make a successful stand against the attacking army. In this case the advantages generally aimed at are to threaten or sever the communications of the enemy, and to force him to fight a battle where a defeat will ruin his army. From the foregoing, it is evident that these two methods of attack have a tendency to produce opposite results. A direct attack upon the enemy, if successful, breaks up and scatters his forces. On the other hand, a flank attack gives him a chance to concentrate, but at the same time places him in a position where a defeat will ruin him.

In making a choice between these two methods of attack, the able general will be guided in great measure by the positions occupied by the enemy's forces. But, as a rule, if he adopt one method, he must abandon the advantages to be derived from the other. Thus, should he decide to attack the centre of the enemy's line, he may reasonably expect to divide the forces of the enemy, and afterwards to defeat them in detail; but he cannot expect to threaten at the same time their communications, and cut them from their base of operations. On the other hand, if he make a flank attack, he may reasonably expect to sever the communications of the enemy, and thus force him to fight a battle under disadvantageous circumstances; but he cannot expect to defeat in turn the several parts of the enemy's army.

But in the campaign between Moreau and Kray, it is a remarkable fact that the positions of the Austrian forces were such that the advantages of both a front and flank attack could be obtained by the French. By crossing the Rhine at Schaffhausen, and by attacking the flank of Kray in the Black Forest, the French would not only separate the Austrian left from the Austrian centre and right, but would threaten the Austrian communications with Ulm. From the beginning Bonaparte saw clearly this fact. His eye took in the entire situation. Thus it was that he was anxious to have Moreau undertake this movement. Thus it was that he himself had thought seriously at one time of uniting the Army of Reserve with the Army of the Rhine, and of moving against the left flank of Kray's forces in the Black Forest.

From this discussion, it is evident that, had Moreau made no errors, even after he assembled his three corps near Schaffhausen, he could have brought superior numbers upon every battle-field in Germany, and thus have won more decisive victories and have accomplished far greater results. What, then, might not Bonaparte himself have accomplished had he directed in person one hundred and seventy thousand soldiers against the one hundred and twenty thousand Austrians in Germany? When it is remembered that he never lost a battle in which he was superior to his adversary in numbers, it cannot be doubted what the result would have been.

CHAPTER IV.

MARENGO.[1]

ANXIOUSLY Bonaparte at Paris awaited the success of the Army of the Rhine. Matters were urgent and time was precious, for Masséna could hold out but a few days longer at Genoa. Until the French should be victorious in Germany, the First Consul could not expect Moreau to send a detachment across Switzerland into Italy. As soon as word should be brought that this re-enforcement was on its way, Bonaparte purposed to lead the Army of Reserve across the Alps against Melas, who was fighting the French so vigorously at Genoa and along the Var.

On the 6th of May Bonaparte left Paris to direct the operations of the Army of Reserve. He had already assembled the several parts of that army near Lake Geneva, and had collected vast supplies there, which were to be used by the army in its march into Italy. On his arrival at Dijon, he reviewed the few thousand conscripts and old soldiers at that place. After this review,

---

[1] See Maps 2 and 4.

which was intended to confirm the spies still further in their belief that the Army of Reserve was purely imaginary, he proceeded to Geneva, and thence to Lausanne, at which places the greater part of the army was assembled. On his arrival there, Bonaparte began the final preparations for crossing the Alps. At first, he thought of leading the Army of Reserve into Switzerland, in order to unite it with Moncey's corps, which had been detached from the Army of the Rhine, and thence march through the St. Gothard Pass into Italy. He also considered the plan of marching into Switzerland, and thence of descending into Italy by way of the Simplon Pass. But after receiving the report of General Marescot, who had been sent to examine the several passes of the Alps, he decided to conduct the greater part of his forces over the Great St. Bernard Pass. By taking this route, which was much the shortest, he could reach Milan earlier, and thus gain the great advantage of time.

The plan of Bonaparte was to conduct thirty-five thousand men of the Army of Reserve over this pass into Italy, and to send the remaining five thousand over the Little St. Bernard Pass, which lies in the Alps but a few miles south of the Great St. Bernard. At the same time a small detachment was to proceed from Switzerland into Italy by way of the Simplon Pass; and Thurreau's division of four thousand, which formed the left of the

Army of Italy, was to descend from the Mont Cenis Pass and attack the Austrians in the vicinity of Turin.   These movements having been accomplished, Bonaparte intended to direct the greater part of the Army of Reserve on Milan, where it was to unite with Moncey's corps, which was marching over the St. Gothard into Italy.   Should this part of the plan be successfully executed, Bonaparte then purposed to march south with a strong force, cross the Po near Placentia, and occupy the Stradella Pass.   This pass, which is enclosed on the north by the Po and on the south by the spurs that shoot northward from the main chain of the Apennines, is a strong position on the direct road between Alessandria and Mantua. While holding the pass, Bonaparte expected to debouch westward therefrom against Melas, who, he calculated, would advance eastward from Alessandria and meet him in the plains of the Scrivia.

It is clear, from the histories of this campaign, that the plan as here set forth had not been determined on in all its details before the movements began.   In fact, until Bonaparte descended the eastern slope of the Alps, he had not fully decided whether he would march directly on Milan, or on Alessandria and the fortress of Tortona, in order thus to bring relief more quickly to Masséna. Circumstances would then determine the matter. But there is little doubt that before leaving Paris he had mapped out in his own mind the essential features of the plan as here set forth. Upon this point Bourrienne, in his "Memoirs of Napoleon Bonaparte," writes as follows: —

"On the 17th of March, in a moment of gaiety and good humor, he (Bonaparte) desired me to unroll Chauchard's great map of Italy. He lay down upon it and desired me to do likewise. He then stuck into it pins, the heads of which were tipped with wax, some red and some black. I silently observed him, and awaited with no little curiosity the result of this plan of campaign. When he had stationed the enemy's corps, and drawn up the pins with the red heads on the points where he hoped to bring his own troops, he said to me, 'Where do you think I shall beat Melas?' — 'How the devil should I know?' — 'Why, look here, you fool; Melas is at Alessandria with his headquarters. There he will remain until Genoa surrenders. He has in Alessandria his magazines, his hospitals, his artillery, and his reserves. Crossing the Alps here' (pointing to the Great Mont St. Bernard) 'I shall fall upon Melas, cut off his communications with Austria, and meet him here in the plains of the Scrivia' (placing a red pin at San Giuliano). Finding that I looked on this manœuvre of pins as mere pastime, he addressed to me some of his usual compliments, such as fool, ninny, etc., and then proceeded to demonstrate his plans more clearly on the map."

The correspondence of Bonaparte at this time shows that he had a full knowledge of the positions and condition of the Austrian forces in Italy. From information sent him by Suchet, he learned that the Austrian army was greatly scattered; that but a small portion of it was occupying that part of northern Italy between the Po and Switzerland; and that as yet General Melas did not believe in the existence of the Army of Reserve. It was this knowledge which caused the First Consul to believe that he could execute successfully this bold and hazardous undertaking.

From Villeneuve, at the east end of Lake Geneva, the road across the Alps into Italy passes through the towns of Martigny and Saint Pierre, thence over the Great St. Bernard, through the village of Saint Remy, into the valley of the Aosta, and thence it continues along the Dora Baltea River, through the towns of Aosta, Châtillon, Bard, and Ivrea, into the plains of Piedmont. Not far south of the Great St. Bernard lies the Little St. Bernard Pass, which opens also into the valley of the Aosta. In 1800 these two roads were much more difficult of passage than they are at the present time. When Bonaparte crossed the Alps, the road from Saint Pierre to Saint Remy was simply a bridle path over which no vehicle could pass. Even now it would be a hazardous undertaking to conduct a large army into Italy over the Great St. Bernard. Crossing the Alps at an elevation of more than eight thousand feet, the pass lies in a region of perpetual snow and ice, where the glaciers, the shock of avalanches, and the frequent and blinding storms make the passage of troops difficult and dangerous.

Having once reached the fertile valley of the

Po, Bonaparte expected to find food and forage there in abundance; but during the march from Villeneuve to Ivrea it was necessary to provide supplies in advance for the army. For this purpose he had collected them at Lake Geneva. He now caused them to be distributed at different points along this route. He also sent money to the monks in charge of the Great St. Bernard Hospital, in order that they should purchase bread, cheese, and wine for the soldiers. At Villeneuve, Martigny, Saint Pierre, and Saint Remy, he established hospitals for the sick and injured. To the foot of the defile at Saint Pierre he sent forward a company of mechanics to dismount the guns and to divide the gun-carriages and caissons into numbered parts for transportation on pack mules. The ammunition too was carried in this way. But the cannon themselves could not be thus transported. For this purpose sledges with rollers had been made, but they were found to be of no use. Finally, the cannon were enclosed within the trunks of trees hollowed out for the purpose. Thus protected, they were dragged across the Alps by the soldiers themselves. A second company of mechanics was ordered to march with the first division and to establish itself at Saint Remy, in order to put together the carriages and caissons, to remount the pieces, and to make the necessary repairs.

On the 14th of May Bonaparte was ready to begin the movement. The Army of Reserve numbered forty thousand soldiers and forty cannon; about four thousand were cavalry. Four corps of the army, numbering thirty-five thousand men, commanded by Murat, Victor, Duhesme, and Lannes, had taken position from Villeneuve to Saint Pierre. A fifth corps, of five thousand men, commanded by Chabran, was in Savoy at the foot of the Little St. Bernard Pass. Bonaparte himself was at Martigny, at which place he issued the orders for the movement. He had sent Berthier forward to receive the divisions on the Italian side of the Alps.

On the 15th of May the movement began. Lannes crossed first. He began his march from Saint Pierre at two o'clock in the morning, in order to avoid as much as possible the danger from the avalanches, which are less frequent in the cool of the day. He reached the summit safely, and his soldiers were pleasantly surprised to find there the bread, cheese, and wine which Bonaparte had provided for them. Lannes halted but a moment at the Great St. Bernard Hospital; he then began the descent and arrived at Saint Remy on the same day. He was followed in turn by the corps in his rear. At the same time Chabran crossed the Little St. Bernard Pass, and Thurreau began to advance over the Mont Cenis Pass. The entire Army of Reserve crossed between the 15th and 20th of May. During this famous passage of the Alps the soldiers were filled with energy and enthusiasm. Though heavily laden, they themselves, by sheer strength, dragged their cannon over the rough and slippery paths. No exertion seemed to tire them. As they pressed on, all were gay and cheerful. As they climbed the mountain side, their spirits rose. With shouts and cheers and songs, they made that Alpine region ring. In that cold, clear air they felt their blood quicken. They felt, too, the energy, the enthusiasm, the magnetism, of their commander. They not only hoped for, but they expected victory. Were they not imitating the daring deeds of the great Hannibal? Were they not about to enter that Italy where their comrades had fought so gloriously before? Were they not commanded by the "Little Corporal," their idol, whose deeds of desperate daring at the bridges of Lodi and Arcole had won their everlasting admiration?

Thus the Army of Reserve crossed the Alps. By the 20th of May all five corps had reached the valley of the Aosta. Owing to the careful preparations made, there had been scarcely any accidents and no serious delays during the passage. But the greatest difficulty was yet to be met. Some distance down the valley of the Aosta, upon a perpendicular rock commanding a narrow defile, Fort Bard had been constructed. Though this fort was garrisoned by only two or three hundred Austrians, it was impregnable and controlled the whole val-

ley. After descending the Great St. Bernard Pass,
Lannes had pushed on down the valley, but was
stopped by the fire of the fort. At once he made
an effort to capture the place, but was repulsed.
He soon saw that it could not be taken by force.
Though he gained the road that led past the fort,
the deadly fire of the Austrians prevented him
from advancing. For a time it seemed that this
small but formidable fort would stop the progress
of the whole army. Lannes was greatly disturbed.
He reported the matter to Berthier, and Berthier
sent at once a courier to inform Bonaparte of the
situation. The First Consul was still at Martigny,
where he had remained for the purpose of hastening forward all the artillery and the rear divisions
of the army. This news was a complete surprise
to Bonaparte. The effect which it produced upon
him is thus described by Thiers : —

"This announcement of an obstacle, considered insurmountable at first, made a terrible impression on
him ; but he recovered quickly, and refused positively
to admit the possibility of a retreat. Nothing in the
world should reduce him to such an extremity. He
thought that, if one of the loftiest mountains of the globe
had failed to arrest his progress, a secondary rock could
not be capable of vanquishing his courage and his genius.
The fort, said he to himself, might be taken by bold
courage ; if it could not be taken, it still could be turned.
Besides, if the infantry and cavalry could pass it, with but a
few four-pounders, they could then proceed to Ivrea at the
mouth of the gorge, and wait until their heavy guns could

follow them. And if the heavy guns could not pass the obstacle which had arisen, and if, in order to get any, those of the enemy had to be taken, the French infantry were brave and numerous enough to assail the Austrians and take their cannon.

"Moreover, he studied his maps again and again, questioned a number of Italian officers, and learning from them that many other roads led from Aosta to the neighboring valleys, he wrote letter after letter to Berthier, forbidding him to stop the progress of the army, and pointing out to him with wonderful precision what reconnoissances should be made around the fort of Bard."

Having sent these instructions to Berthier and having seen the last division well on its way, the First Consul hurried across the Alps towards Fort Bard. Meanwhile a foot-path, leading along the mountain side around the fort, was discovered by Lannes. By a few repairs the path was soon rendered passable for the men and horses, but not for the artillery. How to get the cannon past the fort was the question. Finally, the following method was adopted. During a dark night the road in front of the fort was strewn with manure and straw, and, to deaden the sound of the artillery wheels, they were wrapped with tow and straw; then the soldiers themselves quietly hauled the guns past the fort. The stratagem succeeded; all the artillery was thus transported. In this way the Army of Reserve surmounted this obstacle, which for a time gave Bonaparte greater anxiety than the passage of the Great St. Bernard itself.

At this time the lower valley of the Aosta was guarded. by three thousand Austrians under General Haddick. On the 20th of May Lannes arrived at Ivrea, which was occupied by the enemy. He attacked the Austrian garrison there, defeated it, and captured the place. Thence, continuing his march towards Chivasso, he again attacked the Austrians on the Chiusella, defeated them, drove them from position to position, and finally, having forced them back towards Turin, captured Chivasso. Meanwhile Bonaparte, having left Chabran's corps to blockade Fort Bard, followed Lannes with the remainder of the army.

During these operations, General Thurreau descended the Mont Cenis Pass and attacked General Kaim, who, with five thousand men, was at Susa guarding the Mont Cenis route into Italy. Before the spirited attacks of Thurreau, Kaim was obliged to abandon Susa and fall back to Busseleno on the road to Turin.

On the 27th of May Bonaparte with the greater part of the Army of Reserve was near Chivasso, Thurreau was at Susa, a French detachment, under Bethencourt, was descending the Simplon Pass, and Moncey's corps was struggling heroically towards Milan over the St. Gothard. Thus far the plans of the First Consul had been successful. He had crossed the Alps, forced his way past Fort Bard, and driven the enemy out of the valley of the Aosta. Now, the thunder of his cannon could be heard on the plains of Piedmont. But what of the Austrians! Where were they? Where was Melas?

Still incredulous as to the existence of an army of reserve, Melas was bending every energy to capture Genoa and to force the crossings of the Var. In the engagements and battles with Masséna and Suchet, the army of Melas, which originally numbered one hundred and twenty thousand, had been reduced to one hundred thousand men. These troops were greatly scattered. On the 13th of May they were thus stationed: thirty thousand under General Ott were besieging Genoa; twenty-five thousand under General Elsnitz were fighting Suchet along the Var; ten thousand under General Vukassovich were watching the Italian entrances of the St. Gothard and Simplon passes; three thousand, commanded by General Haddick, were in the lower valley of the Aosta, watching the St. Bernard passes; five thousand, commanded by General Kaim, were occupying Susa at the foot of the Mont Cenis Pass; and two thousand were scattered along the Maritime Alps near the Tenda Pass. In addition, six thousand were on their way from Tuscany to re-enforce Melas; three thousand remained in Tuscany, and sixteen thousand more occupied Alessandria, the fortresses of Tortona and Mantua, and various other garrisons of northern Italy.

Such was the situation of the Austrians when,

on the 21st of May, Melas received information of
the passage of French troops over the Great St.
Bernard.   Immediately he collected ten thousand
soldiers from the Austrian forces in front of Suchet
and in the vicinity of the Tenda Pass, and marched
on Turin.   At first, he believed that the French
troops appearing in Italy were merely a detachment sent thither to harass his rear; but at Coni,
where he arrived on the 22d of May, he learned
to a certainty that Bonaparte himself was in Italy;
that the French soldiers were already issuing into
the plains of Piedmont; and that the First Consul
had with him both cannon and cavalry.   Melas
was surprised.   He knew not what to do.   Having
been repeatedly informed by his own spies, and
even by the Aulic Council, that the Army of Reserve was a mere fiction, he could now hardly bring
himself to believe that it was a reality.   It might,
after all, be but a large detachment; for how could
Bonaparte cross the Alps with an army?   How
could he pass Fort Bard with cannon and cavalry?
It must be remembered, too, that at this time
Melas had not learned that Moncey was marching
on Milan.   As yet, therefore, he was not completely
undeceived.   He knew that a French force was at
the foot of the Mont Cenis Pass, and that French
troops were issuing from the valley of the Aosta
into the plains of Piedmont; but he did not know
the number of the French forces nor did he know
the intentions of Bonaparte.   Consequently he de-

layed issuing the orders for the concentration of his scattered troops.

Having reached Turin with ten thousand men, Melas was joined by General Haddick's command, which had been driven from the valley of the Aosta by Lannes, and by General Kaim's division, which had been driven from Susa by Thurreau. But this junction gave Melas only sixteen or seventeen thousand Austrians to oppose the thirty-five thousand French near Chivasso under Bonaparte.

At this time Melas expected the French to cross the Po and attack him near Turin; but such was not the intention of Bonaparte. In order to deceive Melas, the First Consul ordered Lannes to make preparations as if the French intended to cross the Po at Chivasso, then to march rapidly down the river, through Crescentino and Candia, on Pavia. At the same time Bonaparte himself, with the corps of Victor, Duhesme, and Murat, set out for Milan by way of Vercelli and Novara. On the 31st of May Bonaparte arrived at the Ticino River. To oppose the passage of the French, Vukassovich had collected a considerable force on the east bank. Bonaparte crossed the river, attacked and defeated the Austrians, thence, continuing his march eastward, entered Milan on the 2d of June. Vukassovich, having left a garrison in the castle of Milan, fell back behind the Adda. At Milan Bonaparte

delayed several days to await the arrival of
Moncey's corps, the advance guard of which was
just beginning to appear in Italy.   During the
delay Bonaparte directed a part of his forces on
Brescia, Lodi, and Cremona.   As a result of
these movements, Vukassovich retired behind the
Mincio and sought safety under the guns of
Mantua.   Bonaparte also directed Murat on
Placentia in order to seize the crossings of the Po
there.

Meanwhile the detachment under Bethencourt,
marching by way of the Simplon Pass, had
reached Arona at the lower end of Lake Maggiore.
On the 1st of June Fort Bard surrendered to
Chabran.   Having left a garrison in this place,
and one also in Ivrea, he then took up a position
with the remainder of his corps along the Po from
Chivasso to the Sesia River.   From the Sesia to
Pavia the corps of Lannes occupied the line of
the Po.   On the 1st of June Lannes had captured
this place, and had seized the large magazines
there, which contained provisions, several pieces
of artillery, and a number of pontoon boats.

Thus it will be seen that the French were in
possession of the whole of northern Italy lying
between the Po and Switzerland.   Looking south
from Milan, Bonaparte had in his front the line
of the Po, which he held from Chivasso to
Cremona.   Far away to his right was the Great
St. Bernard Pass, which he had just crossed, and

which was now guarded by the French garrisons
of Fort Bard and Ivrea. To his left, at a distance
of eighty miles, was the Mincio, which formed
on that side the dividing line between the French
and the Austrians; and in his rear were the St.
Gothard and Simplon passes, which offered him a
safe retreat into Switzerland in case he should
meet with a reverse. Already, within this territory, he had seized all the Austrian communications, captured several Austrian garrisons,
occupied several cities, and taken possession of
immense quantities of provisions and munitions
of war.

Thus situated, Bonaparte was almost ready to
strike the blow that should decide the fate of
Italy. In a few days he would cross the Po,
march through the Stradella Pass, and encounter
Melas on the bloody field of Marengo. The delay
at Milan was but the lull before the storm. While
Bonaparte remained there, completing his arrangements and awaiting the arrival of Moncey, Melas
was beginning to appreciate the situation, and,
though still somewhat confused and undecided,
was destined shortly to make an heroic effort to
save his army.

For several days after Melas reached Turin,
he remained in doubt as to the intentions of
Bonaparte. In fact, he was deceived by the preparations that Lannes had made to cross the Po
at Chivasso. Again: in descending the river

towards Pavia, Lannes so masked the main part of
the Army of Reserve, that Melas did not immediately become aware of the movement on Milan.
But on the 29th of May he learned that Bonaparte
was marching on Milan; and, on the 31st, he
learned that Moreau had defeated Kray, and that
Moncey's corps was marching by way of the St.
Gothard into Italy.   At once he comprehended
the vast plan of Bonaparte.   He saw that nothing
could now prevent the Army of Reserve from
uniting with Moncey's corps; and that, with
these combined forces, Bonaparte would doubtless
march south from Milan, cross the Po, and sever
the Austrian communications.   Thus he saw himself being rapidly enclosed in a net from which
there would soon be little or no hope of escape.
Being now completely undeceived as to the intentions of Bonaparte, Melas had no further cause for
delay.   He must concentrate his troops at once,
in order to break through the French forces
rapidly closing in upon him.   He must, if possible, preserve his communications, and thus save
his army from capture or annihilation.

Accordingly, he determined to concentrate at
Placentia and the Stradella Pass all the available
Austrian troops that were fighting the French
near Genoa.   By this means he hoped to seize
and hold the crossings of the Po from Pavia to
Cremona, and thus to retain possession of the
great highway leading from Alessandria through

the Stradella Pass to Mantua. He also determined
to unite at Alessandria all the available Austrian
troops in Piedmont and along the Var. By this
means he expected to assemble there an army of
at least thirty thousand men, and thence to proceed eastward through the Stradella Pass to
Mantua. By following this plan, he hoped to
make his escape with the greater part of his
army. Having once reached the Mincio, he
could unite his forces with those of Vukassovich;
and, perhaps, in this strong position, flanked on
one side by Lake Garda, and on the other by the
fortress of Mantua, he might be able to make a
successful stand against Bonaparte.

In accordance with this plan, he sent impera-
tive orders to General Elsnitz to quit the Var and
march on Alessandria, and to General Ott to
raise the siege of Genoa and hasten north in
order to seize Placentia and the crossings of
the Po near that point. Meanwhile he himself,
having left a sufficient force to hold Thurreau in
check, hastened with the remainder of his army
to march on Alessandria.

Upon receiving the orders of Melas, General
Elsnitz, whose command then numbered but
seventeen thousand, began to withdraw his forces
from the Var. He directed his columns towards
the Tenda Pass, expecting to cross the Apennines
at that point, and thence to march on Alessandria
by way of Coni, Alba, and Asti. But Suchet,

being well aware of the desperate situation of
Melas, was anticipating the recall of Elsnitz and
was prepared for it. Suchet's forces numbered
fourteen thousand men. By skilful manœuvring
and by a rapid march across the foothills of the
Apennines, he succeeded in reaching the Tenda
Pass ahead of his adversary. Having thus turned
the flank of the Austrians, and obtained possession of their line of retreat, he fell upon them,
defeated them, cut them in two, and killed,
wounded, or captured more than half of their
army. As a result General Elsnitz was compelled
to retreat eastward and cross the Apennines over
the Ormea Pass. With only eight thousand men
he arrived at Ceva on the 7th of June *en route* to
Alessandria. Meanwhile Suchet, having proceeded eastward to Savona, was joined by a part
of Masséna's command, which had marched out of
Genoa on the 5th of June. With these combined
forces, Suchet marched to Acqui, and there, still
acting under the orders of Masséna, awaited the
results of Bonaparte's operations.

When, on the 2d of June, General Ott received
the orders of Melas, the negotiations for the capitulation of Genoa were pending. He delayed until
the 4th of June to receive the surrender of
Masséna. On the 6th, having left a sufficient
force to garrison the city, he sent a brigade
towards Placentia by way of Bobbio; and with
the remainder of his forces, numbering sixteen

thousand soldiers, he himself marched towards the same place by way of Novi, Tortona, and the Stradella Pass.

During these operations, Bonaparte remained at Milan, perfecting his arrangements and issuing the orders for the movements of his troops. He had already sent forward Berthier to direct the operations along the Po. On the 6th of June Moncey's corps arrived. This re-enforcement of fifteen thousand men increased the effective forces under the immediate command of Bonaparte to about sixty thousand. Immediately upon the arrival of Moncey, thirty-two thousand soldiers under Lannes, Victor, and Murat, began to cross the Po. The remainder of the army were thus stationed: four thousand, under Thurreau, were at the foot of the Mont Cenis Pass; two small detachments were occupying Fort Bard and Ivrea; ten thousand were posted at Vercelli and along the Ticino from the foot of Lake Maggiore to Pavia; three thousand were at Milan; and ten thousand were along the Adda, and at Cremona and Placentia. All these troops, except the division of Thurreau, which was isolated and held in check by an Austrian force near Turin, were available for the operations about Milan and along the Po.

On the 6th of June Lannes and Victor crossed the Po near Belgiojoso, a few miles below Pavia, and marched thence to the Stradella Pass. On the following day Murat crossed at Placentia. In these passages the French met with considerable opposition from small detachments of cavalry and infantry that Melas had directed thither from Alessandria and elsewhere to hold the crossings of the Po until General Ott should arrive; but these detachments having been defeated and driven back, the French occupied Placentia and the Stradella Pass. At the latter place a fortified camp was constructed, and between Pavia and Placentia five bridges were built for the use of the French in case they should be forced to retreat.

During these operations two Austrian couriers were captured. One was carrying despatches from Melas to Vienna; the other, from the Aulic Council to Melas. The despatches of the former told of the surrender of Genoa, and of the plans and movements of Melas. Those of the latter informed the Austrian commander that the Army of Reserve was a mere myth, and that he should pay no attention to the rumors concerning it, but should make every effort to capture Genoa and force the crossings of the Var.

The news that Genoa had surrendered was discouraging to Bonaparte, for he at once appreciated the fact that he must now fight the forces of General Ott in addition to those which Melas was assembling at Alessandria. There was, however, a compensating advantage in knowing the plans of his adversary, for, having learned that General Ott was marching on Placentia, he at once saw that he might defeat this corps, and perhaps destroy it, before it could reach Placentia or unite with Melas. Accordingly, he sent to Berthier, Lannes, and Murat the following instructions: "Concentrate yourselves at the Stradella. On the 8th or 9th at the latest, you will have upon your hands fifteen or eighteen thousand Austrians, coming from Genoa. Meet them and cut them to pieces. It will be so many enemies less upon our hands on the day of the decisive battle which we are to expect with the entire army of Melas."

In accordance with these instructions, Lannes and Victor faced about their columns and proceeded westward towards Tortona. Lannes, commanding the vanguard, preceded Victor by a distance of five miles. The remainder of the French forces on the south bank of the Po marched to the Stradella Pass. On the 9th of June Lannes with nine thousand men encountered the sixteen thousand under Ott at Montebello. Immediately a furious battle began. For several hours both sides fought desperately. The Austrian superiority in numbers would have crushed an ordinary soldier, but Lannes was of uncommon mould. Impetuous, stubborn, brave, fierce, and terrible on the battle-field, he would not yield. In the face of a deadly fire he encouraged his soldiers, and by his presence and heroic action held them firm before the repeated onslaughts of the Austrians. Nevertheless, he would eventually have been defeated had not Victor arrived opportunely on the battle-field with six thousand men. This re-enforcement turned the tide of battle in favor of the French. The Austrians were defeated, cut to pieces, and compelled finally to retreat. They lost in killed, wounded, and captured five thousand men; the French, three thousand. With the remnants of his corps General Ott fell back across the Scrivia, and thence proceeded to Alessandria. This battle secured for Lannes the title of "Duke of Montebello." It covered him with glory, and brought to his name an imperishable renown.

The First Consul, who had left Milan on the morning of the 9th of June, arrived at Montebello just at the termination of the battle. Expecting that Melas would at once advance with all the troops that he had collected at Alessandria, Bonaparte began on the 10th of June to rearrange his troops, and to make preparations for battle. Being deficient in both cavalry and artillery, while Melas was well supplied with both, Bonaparte decided to fall back to a position near Casteggio, in front of the Stradella Pass, where his flanks would be protected by the Po on one side, and by the spurs of the Apennines on the other. With the corps of Lannes and Victor he made a retrograde movement to this point. Here he collected all his forces south of the Po, now numbering twenty-nine thousand men. In this strong position he remained for several days, expecting hourly that the Austrians would push forward from Alessandria and attack him. But they failed to appear.

On the 11th of June General Desaix, who had served under Bonaparte in Egypt, arrived at the French headquarters. He was a distinguished general, and a warm friend of the First Consul. At once Bonaparte gave him the command of a corps, consisting of two divisions.

On the following day Bonaparte, surprised at the non-appearance of the Austrians, began to fear that they were trying to escape. He thought that Melas might attempt to evade him, either by marching directly on Genoa, or by crossing the Po at Valenza, and thence marching on Pavia and Milan. Finally, he could bear the suspense no longer. He decided to advance and seek Melas. Accordingly, on the afternoon of the 12th of June, having left a force to occupy the intrenched camp at the Stradella Pass, he advanced towards Alessandria. At Tortona he left a force to block-ade the fortress. On the 13th of June he crossed the Scrivia and debouched into the plain of Marengo, which lies between the Scrivia and Bormida rivers. Thus far he had met with no Austrians. His anxiety increased. He had but few cavalry, and, consequently, was unable to make a thorough reconnoissance of the surrounding country.   During the afternoon of that day, he directed Victor on Marengo.   Here the French found only a small detachment, which was quickly driven across the Bormida.   A party sent forward to reconnoitre the crossings of the Bormida, reported that no Austrians were to be found there in force.

From all these indications, Bonaparte came to the conclusion that the Austrians had left Alessandria.   He reasoned that, if Melas intended to attack the French and force his way through the Stradella Pass, he would neither have given up the plain without a struggle, nor have failed to occupy in force the village of Marengo.   Moreover, he thought that Melas would surely not neglect to hold the Bormida with a strong force so long as he remained at Alessandria.   But if he had gone, what route had he taken?

On that day Bonaparte received word that no Austrians had appeared at Pavia or along the Ticino.   It seemed probable, therefore, that Melas might be marching on Genoa; and that he would attempt either to make a stand there, where he could be supported by the British fleet, or else to march thence through Bobbio, Placentia, and Cremona to Mantua.   With this thought in his mind, Bonaparte directed Desaix with one division of his corps, numbering six thousand men, on Novi, in order to intercept Melas, should he be attempting to escape by this route.

Thus it happened that on the evening of the 13th of June Bonaparte was unprepared for the battle of the next day. His forces were scattered. Desaix was on his way to Novi; Victor was at Marengo; Lannes and Murat were on the plain in rear of Victor; the Consular Guard, two regiments of cavalry, and Monnier's division, which belonged to the corps of Desaix, were along the Scrivia near Tortona. These forces numbered twenty-eight thousand men, of whom three thousand and five hundred were cavalry. Bonaparte had about forty cannon. That night he slept in a small town about two miles east of San Giuliano. He expected to receive on the next day some information that would enlighten him as to the movements and intentions of Melas; but he had no thought of a battle on the morrow.

Meanwhile, at Alessandria there was much confusion. By the defeat of General Ott at Montebello, Melas had lost possession of the direct road from Alessandria through the Stradella Pass to Mantua. He could not, therefore, make his escape by this route without first defeating the French. He hardly knew what to do. Already his communications were severed. Doubtless the French would soon advance towards Alessandria. Perhaps, in a few days, they would force the crossings of the Bormida, and attempt to shut him up within the city. In this uncertain state of mind Melas called a council of war. To the officers composing the council three plans suggested themselves. Should they cross the Po at Valenza, march to Pavia, and attempt to make their escape by forcing their way across the Ticino; or should they march to Genoa, and in that place, supported by the British fleet, make preparations to stand a siege; or, lastly, should they cross the Bormida, meet the French face to face, and fight to recover their communications and save their army?

The third plan was adopted. The Austrian officers reasoned that it was doubtful whether either of the first two plans would succeed; that the false position that they now occupied was due neither to Melas nor to themselves, but to the Aulic Council, which had repeatedly misinformed them as to the actual state of affairs; and that now the only honorable course was to fight, and, if possible, cut their way through the French forces. "If we succeed," said they, "victory will regain for us the road to Placentia and Mantua; if not, we shall have done our duty, and the responsibility of any disaster that may befall us will rest upon other heads than ours."

Melas concurred in the views of his officers. Though seventy years old, age had not dimmed his courage. His army at Alessandria numbered thirty-two thousand men, and contained two hundred pieces of artillery and seven thousand cavalry.

On the 13th of June he decided that on the next day he would cross the Bormida and attack Bonaparte.

The plain of Marengo lies between the Scrivia and Bormida rivers, which rise in the Apennines and flow northward towards the Po. The town of Marengo, from which this battle takes its name, is situated near the east bank of the Bormida on the great highway leading from Alessandria to Mantua. About two miles north of Marengo is the village of Castel-ceriolo. On the main road, just east of Alessandria, two bridges span the Bormida. They were held by the Austrians, and were defended by a single bridge-head on the right bank. The surrounding country is generally quite flat, but towards the village of San Giuliano, which lies on the main road about three miles east of Marengo, several hillocks thereabout render the ground uneven.

At daybreak on the morning of the 14th of June, the Austrians began to cross the Bormida and to issue from the bridge-head on the right bank. Three thousand soldiers under General O'Reilly crossed first. They drove back the French outposts and advanced towards Marengo. This vanguard was followed by a division under Haddick, and that in turn by another under Kaim. At eight o'clock these forces, having deployed, began the battle. Being well supplied with cannon, they opened the attack with a heavy artillery fire, then pressed forward towards Marengo.

Meanwhile, word was sent to Bonaparte that the whole Austrian army was advancing. During the deployment of the Austrians, Victor at Marengo had taken up a position in front of the village along the muddy stream of Fontanone. Here he received the attacks of the Austrians, and finally succeeded in driving them back. But the Austrian line was soon strongly re-enforced. Melas directed two more divisions on Marengo, and, having detached Ott's division, directed it on Castel-ceriolo, in order to take the French in flank on that side.

About ten o'clock Lannes brought his corps into line on the right of Victor. He was supported by a cavalry brigade under Champeaux. Kellerman's brigade of cavalry supported Victor. Meanwhile General Ott, having arrived near Castel-ceriolo, began to threaten the French right, which movement obliged Lannes to form front in that direction with a part of his corps. The French line of battle, numbering about fifteen thousand men, was about two miles long. It followed the general direction of the Fontanone northward from Marengo towards Castel-ceriolo, and westward from Marengo towards the Bormida. Facing this line were the Austrian troops, numbering twenty-nine thousand five hundred men. General Ott formed the left, and the reserve under General Elsnitz was in the rear. Having been informed that Suchet had reached Acqui, Melas had, during the morning, sent two thousand five hundred of his reserve cavalry to reconnoitre in that direction.

At ten o'clock Melas attacked with fury the whole French line. He made a determined effort to drive back Victor's corps and to gain possession of Marengo. Along the stream in front of the village the struggle was fierce and bloody. Both sides fought desperately. Melas felt that he *must* conquer. Knowing that his situation was critical, and that nothing short of victory could save his army, he fought with the courage of despair. The French, too, fought like demons. Their victory at Montebello had encouraged them; and now, having sought and found their enemy, they expected to be again triumphant. With determination they resisted the onsets of Melas. Before the furious attacks of superior numbers, in the face of cannon, sabre, and steel, they stood to their work like men. But all their efforts were unavailing. Against so fierce an attack Victor could not long hold his position. He was compelled to fall back to Marengo, where he again made a desperate effort to stop the advance of the Austrians. For a time he held on to the village, but was finally forced to give way. His corps was routed; his soldiers became demoralized. In disorder they retired towards San Giuliano, followed

by the victorious Austrians.   Meanwhile, Lannes
had held his position against the attacks of Melas
in his front and of Ott on his right.   But when
Victor gave way, Lannes found himself in a
desperate situation.   This movement uncovered
the left of his corps and threatened it with destruction.   Thus outflanked on both wings and hard
pressed in front, he saw defeat near at hand.   In
fact the Austrians were on the point of sweeping
everything before them.   Though the French were
still fighting bravely, it was evident that they
must soon fall back into the plain, or else be
routed and destroyed.

Such was the situation at eleven o'clock when
Bonaparte arrived.   Having received word early
in the morning that the whole Austrian army was
advancing towards Marengo, he immediately sent
Desaix orders to return, then hurried to the front
with all the troops that he could collect.   He
brought with him the Consular Guard, Monnier's
division, and two regiments of cavalry, — in all
about seven thousand men.   A single glance
sufficed to show Bonaparte what should be done.
He formed the Consular Guard into squares to
hold the Austrian cavalry in check, directed a
column on Castel-ceriolo, sent the greater part of
Monnier's division to re-enforce Lannes, and
ordered Murat with the reserve cavalry to protect
as best he could the retreat of Victor's corps.
Again the struggle was renewed with increased

fury; but all the efforts of Bonaparte and of
Lannes could not now turn the tide of battle in
favor of the French. With an almost resistless
momentum, Melas pressed forward. Seeing victory just within his grasp, he strained every nerve
to crush and annihilate his adversary. He ordered
his reserves to the front and threw them into the
fight. Repeatedly his cavalry charged the French,
cut in on their flanks, and threatened them with
destruction; and, while the left of his line was
resisting bravely the heroic efforts of Lannes, he
himself issued from Marengo with his victorious
troops, and directed them upon the flank of the
French.

It was no longer possible for Bonaparte to hold
his ground. He ordered a retreat. Again the
heroism of Lannes displayed itself on that san-
guinary field. Fighting as he retired, he fell
back slowly and in admirable order. For more
than two hours he prolonged the conflict, while
being forced back from position to position over
a distance of nearly two miles. But, finally, his
indomitable spirit was compelled to yield. His
corps was driven from the field. At length,
shattered, crushed, almost demoralized, it retired behind the hillocks near San Giuliano,
where the remnants of Victor's corps had
assembled.

The Austrians had conquered. On the plain of
Marengo Melas had defeated Bonaparte. The

victory seemed complete. There appeared to be no longer any hope for Bonaparte. The French had been driven three miles beyond Marengo. The greater part of their cavalry had been destroyed. More than two thirds of their cannon had been captured. Fragments only of their infantry organizations remained. On that bloody field six thousand French soldiers had been killed, wounded, or captured. Such was the result of the struggle at Marengo on the morning of the 14th of June, 1800. Who would have thought that before the close of that eventful day the vanquished would become the victors?

Thus far Melas had exhibited great energy and courage; but when the French had been driven from the field, and the excitement of the conflict had ended, he felt deeply the effects of his exertion. The weight of years, too, bore heavily upon him. Fully convinced that he had gained a complete victory over Bonaparte, he left the command of the army to his chief of staff, General Zach, and, having sent despatches to his government announcing the result, returned to Alessandria exhausted with fatigue.

General Zach now rearranged his troops for the purpose of following the French, whom he believed to be completely routed. But the Austrians were not in a condition to pursue the enemy promptly and vigorously. Their cavalry, in particular, had been roughly handled by Victor and Lannes during the morning; and, moreover, it was much weakened by the two thousand five hundred men that Melas had detached towards Acqui to observe Suchet. Considerable time was therefore spent in perfecting the arrangements of Zach. In fact, it was near four o'clock when he began to advance. At the head of about five thousand Austrians he pushed forward along the high-road leading from Marengo to San Giuliano. He was followed at a distance of three quarters of a mile by the corps of Kaim, and it in turn by the Hungarian infantry. At the same time General Ott marched eastward from Castel-ceriolo towards Ghilina. The Austrian troops were only partially deployed. Not expecting great resistance, they were moving forward in marching order rather than in order of battle.

Meanwhile the French, not being vigorously pursued, had halted, and, unperceived by the Austrians, had begun to rally behind the hillocks near San Giuliano. At this time Bonaparte was awaiting anxiously the arrival of Desaix. Early in the morning he had sent him an order to return; but before it reached its destination Desaix, having heard the sound of the first cannon-shot at Marengo, halted his division. Judging from the thunder of the guns that a battle had begun between the French and Austrians on the plain of Marengo, he hurriedly despatched several cavalry troops to Novi, in order to assure himself that no Austrians were in that vicinity, then faced about his troops and marched to the sound of the cannon. Hour after hour he pushed eagerly forward. At about four o'clock in the afternoon the head of his column appeared near San Giuliano.

Upon the arrival of Desaix Bonaparte's spirits rose. Though most of the French officers favored a retreat, Bonaparte was opposed to this course. Desaix, too, concurred in the views of the First Consul. In fact, Desaix was anxious to renew the struggle. Though he saw that the battle was lost, he did not despair of yet gaining another.

Accordingly, Bonaparte at once formed Desaix's division, and the French troops about San Giuliano, into line of battle. Desaix's division was placed across the highway along which the Austrians were advancing. On his right were Lannes, Monnier, and the Consular Guard; in his rear was Victor. Kellerman's brigade of cavalry took a position to the left and rear of Desaix, and Champeaux's brigade to the right and rear of Lannes. Bonaparte had only twelve guns remaining. He placed them on the right of Desaix towards the front of the battle-line.

Such were the positions of the French, when suddenly there appeared from behind the rising ground in their front the column of Zach. Though this column was preceded by an advance

guard with cavalry on each flank, the greater part
of the Austrian troops were marching somewhat
carelessly, and were surprised when they came
thus unexpectedly upon the whole French army
in position for battle. Immediately, the French
guns opened upon Zach; at the same time Desaix
made a furious assault upon him. Kellerman,
too, having been directed towards the right and
rear of Desaix's division during the early stages
of the battle, then moved forward past the right
of Desaix and attacked vigorously the Austrian
cavalry. Having routed it, he wheeled his troop-
ers to the left and struck in flank the Austrian
column, which was already much shaken by the
assault of Desaix. Everywhere the Austrians
were overwhelmed; two thousand were captured,
among whom was General Zach himself. Bonaparte now pushed eagerly forward with his entire
force, and in turn attacked and defeated the corps
of Kaim and the Hungarian infantry. Continuing to advance, he forced the Austrians back to
Marengo. Here they attempted to make a stand,
but were again defeated and routed. In disorder
they retired towards Alessandria.

Meanwhile General Ott, hearing the firing
towards Marengo, marched in that direction; but
he only arrived in time to cover the retreat of the
main body across the Bormida. By ten o'clock
that night all the Austrian troops had recrossed
the river. Thus Bonaparte won in the afternoon

the battle that he had lost in the morning.   Thus a great disaster was turned into a great victory. Once more the Austrians were crushed; once more the French were triumphant.

On the following morning, Bonaparte made preparations to assault the bridge-head and to cross the Bormida, in order to attack the Austrians in Alessandria.   But in the meantime Melas sent an officer to the French headquarters to propose terms of surrender.   On the same day, the 15th of June, the negotiations were completed, and an armistice between Melas and Bonaparte was signed.   By the terms of surrender Melas was allowed to march out of Alessandria with the honors of war, and to proceed thence to Mantua; in return, he was to evacuate the whole of northern Italy as far as the Mincio, to surrender the fortresses of Coni, Alessandria, Genoa, and Tortona, and the fortified cities of Milan, Turin, Pizzighettone, Placentia, Ceva, Savona, and Arona.

In proportion to the number of combatants at Marengo the losses on both sides were large. Seven thousand Austrians were killed or wounded, and three thousand were captured.   The French loss in killed and wounded was equal to that of the Austrians, but only one thousand were captured.   Among the first of the French soldiers killed in the battle of the afternoon was Desaix. While gallantly leading his division against the

Austrians he was shot through the body and fell
dead on the battle-field. His loss was deeply felt
by the First Consul and by the French nation.

On the 15th of May Bonaparte had begun the
passage of the Great St. Bernard with the Army
of Reserve. On the 15th of June he received the
surrender of the Austrian army in Italy. In one
month, he had crossed the Alps, entered Milan,
severed the Austrian communications, fought and
won a great battle, and, as a result, obtained possession of the greater part of northern Italy.

Thus ended the campaign of Marengo. It
brought about a temporary peace between France
and Austria; it excited to a high pitch the military spirit of the French people; and it fixed
ultimately upon the head of Bonaparte an emperor's crown. Upon the political history of
Europe it produced far-reaching results. It pre-
cipitated a contest between England and France,
between France and Europe, which, at irregular
intervals for fifteen years, was destined to continue, until, finally, on the field of Waterloo,
Napoleon's cannon were silenced forever.

COMMENTS.

At the outset one hundred thousand Austrians
were occupying northern Italy. Fifty-five thousand were at Genoa and along the Var; two thousand along the Maritime Alps; five thousand at

the foot of the Mont Cenis Pass; three thousand in the valley of the Aosta; and ten thousand in the vicinity of Milan. The remaining twenty-five thousand were scattered throughout northern Italy. They were engaged mostly in garrisoning the fortresses and fortified cities, and in holding possession of the country.

It will be seen that Melas had so stationed his troops that he was weak at all points. Except at Genoa and along the Var, the Austrian army may be said to have been composed of a number of detachments scattered throughout northern Italy. Melas seemed to think that he must occupy every fortress, and guard every road and pass, in order to make secure his position in Italy. Herein lay his great fault; for, his forces being thus scattered, he could not unite them readily to oppose Bonaparte. Though Melas learned of the march of the Army of Reserve on Milan more than two weeks before the battle of Marengo, yet he was able to assemble only thirty-two thousand men at Alessandria to oppose the French.

The main cause, however, of the defeat of Melas was the fact that he was completely deceived as to the intentions of the First Consul. He had no expectation that Bonaparte would cross the Alps; in fact, he did not believe in the existence of an army of reserve. Having reached this conclusion from the reports of his own spies, and from the instructions sent him by the Aulic

Council, he was utterly confounded when the French descended into Italy from the Mont Cenis, the Great St. Bernard, the Simplon, and St. Gothard passes. Not knowing by which route the strongest column was entering Italy, he knew not where to strike. Consequently, he hesitated and was lost.

Had he fathomed the designs of his adversary in time, he might have rapidly united his forces, and have defeated the several French columns in succession before they could have united in Italy; for, inasmuch as Bonaparte's object was to unite his columns within the Austrian theatre of operations, Melas could concentrate there more quickly than Bonaparte.

On the 29th of May Melas learned of the march of the Army of Reserve on Milan. He then had a splendid opportunity to strike Bonaparte a telling blow. His command at Turin numbered sixteen or seventeen thousand men. In his front at Chivasso and along the Po was Lannes with six or seven thousand. On his left was Thurreau with four thousand. Had Melas left four or five thousand men to hold Thurreau in check, and boldly attacked Lannes with the remainder of his forces, he could easily have defeated Lannes, and have immediately thereafter obtained possession of Bonaparte's communications with France. Such a master stroke would have greatly embarrassed Bonaparte; for he would then have been obliged either to turn back and fight Melas, in order to recover his communications with France, or to push on and fight Vukassovich, in order to establish his communications with Switzerland. Had Bonaparte adopted the former course, Vukassovich could have closed in on the French rear and have thus aided Melas; had he adopted the latter course, Melas could have aided Vukassovich.

That Melas did not carry out this course was due to the fact that no sooner had he learned of the destination of the Army of Reserve than he began to tremble for the safety of his own army. He at once perceived that it was the intention of Bonaparte to sever the Austrian communications. He therefore abandoned any intention which he may have had of attacking Lannes and of seizing the communications of Bonaparte, in order to take the necessary measures for the preservation of his own communications.

Consider now the operations of Bonaparte; they are worthy of careful study. No one who stops to consider the smallness of the means with which he defeated the Austrians in this campaign can fail to appreciate his genius.

At the outset an Austrian army of one hundred thousand men, led by a courageous commander, was in possession of northern Italy. Everywhere Melas had defeated the French. Masséna at Genoa was about to surrender; and Suchet along the Var was fighting desperately to prevent the invasion of France. Melas, encouraged by these successes, looked hopefully forward to new triumphs. Such was the situation when Bonaparte entered Italy with his columns, numbering in all a little less than sixty thousand men. With these forces he plunged into the Austrian theatre of operations, and in a month ended the campaign. He so manoeuvred that a victory of twenty-eight thousand Frenchmen over twenty-nine thousand five hundred Austrians decided the fate of one hundred thousand Austrians and gained for him the greater part of northern Italy.

How, in so short a time and with so few forces, did Bonaparte accomplish such results? In these comments an attempt will be made to answer this question. It is our purpose to analyze somewhat critically the strategical manoeuvres of Bonaparte, to compare the things he did with what he might have done, and to show why the whole of northern Italy fell into his possession as a result of the victory at Marengo. It is our purpose, also, to discuss the battle of Marengo from a tactical point of view, and to set forth some of the reasons why the battle, lost in the morning, was won in the afternoon.

The portion of northern Italy then occupied by the Austrians is divided by the Po and Apennines into three unequal parts, through all which roads pass eastwardly from the French frontier to Mantua. Bonaparte, having decided to lead the

Army of Reserve into Italy, might have adopted any one of three plans. He might have marched into the southern part of the Austrian theatre of operations, lying between the Apennines and the Gulf of Genoa; or into the middle part between the Apennines and the Po; or into the northern part between the Po and Switzerland. Let us examine each of these plans, in order to determine, if possible, which would have procured him the greatest advantages.

Inasmuch as the mountainous and narrow strip of country lying between the Apennines and the sea was peculiarly fitted for the operations of an inferior army, composed mostly of infantry, and inasmuch as the Army of Reserve was deficient in both cavalry and artillery, it might seem that Bonaparte should have united his army with Suchet's forces on the Var for an attack against Melas. But other considerations deterred Bonaparte from doing so. His objections to this course were that even if he succeeded in forcing the crossings of the Var, the Austrians, as they fell back from position to position, would be constantly re-enforced, and could maintain the siege of Genoa. And again: if he succeeded in driving them across the Apennines and in defeating them at Genoa, they could still fall back along their communications to their base of operations on the Mincio, where they would be protected by Lake Garda on one side and by the fortress of

Mantua on the other. Even should the Army of Reserve and all the undefeated portions of the Army of Italy be united into one army, Bonaparte's total strength would not exceed seventy thousand men. With this force he could hardly expect to defeat one hundred thousand Austrians flushed by their recent successes. Furthermore, by adopting this plan, no opportunity would be offered him of severing the Austrian communications.

" An ordinary general," says Jomini, "alarmed by the victorious attitude of the Austrians in Piedmont, would have gone in all haste by Dauphiné toward Provence, and made the Alps the theatre of operations. But Bonaparte appreciated too well the difficulties of a frontal attack. He preferred to cross the mountains upon the rear of the imperial forces and gain the Ticino unopposed, where his presence could not fail to recall his adversaries, and compel them to accept battle with all the chances of success against them."

In order to accomplish this result, Bonaparte had purposely led Melas to believe that the Army of Reserve was intended to re-enforce the Army of Italy. Though Melas did not believe in the existence of an army of reserve, he knew that an effort was being made to organize troops in France, and he believed that they would eventually be sent to join Suchet. But the First

Consul had no intention of doing what Melas expected him to do. It was necessary to the success of Bonaparte that he should conceal as much as possible his own purposes, in order to be able to surprise his adversary. In war it is always wise to lead the enemy to believe that an attack will be made in a different direction from that intended. "In whatever way strategy is employed," says Colonel Maurice, "surprise and concealment are essential to success. On this account it will continually happen, in selecting a line of operations or a scheme of campaign, that the most important point of all is to carry out just what an enemy does not expect. Very often successful campaigns, the method of which has been subsequently much criticised, have owed their success to the fact that, from a nice calculation of time and distance, the successful general has seen that he could carry through an operation dangerous in itself, but sure not to be the one expected by his opponent. For the same reason, in all the brilliant and successful efforts of strategic skill, steps have been taken beforehand to carry out the preliminary movements of an army in such a way as to leave an enemy up to the last moment uncertain in what direction the blow would be struck."

Had Bonaparte marched into the middle part of the Austrian theatre of operations, it would have been necessary to cross the Alps over the Mont

Cenis Pass. The objections to this plan were that the country lying between the Apennines and the Po contained the strong fortifications of Turin, Coni, Alessandria, and Tortona, which would enable the Austrians to hold Bonaparte in check long enough for Melas to concentrate his scattered forces. Furthermore, by entering Italy over this pass, Bonaparte would approach the centre of the Austrian line, which would enable the Austrians to concentrate against him more rapidly than if he moved against either flank of their position. Again: since the Austrians held the passes of the Apennines, they could delay the advance of the French on Genoa and continue the siege; or, if defeated, could fall back along the great highway leading from Piedmont through the Stradella Pass to Mantua.

Though the great chain of the Alps seemed to present an almost impassable barrier to an army attempting to enter the extreme northern part of Italy from France or Switzerland, Bonaparte did not allow this fact to deter him from his great undertaking. There were several reasons why he adopted this plan.

First: He knew that Melas was not expecting the French to enter this part of Italy.

Second: He knew that the country lying between the Po and Switzerland contained but few fortifications, and was occupied by only a few thousand Austrians.

Third: Owing to the fact that he had deceived Melas as to the existence and destination of the Army of Reserve, Bonaparte believed that he could cross the Alps with this army, march to Milan, and there be joined by Moncey's corps before Melas should discover his plan.

Fourth: Inasmuch as all the roads leading from the French frontier to the Austrian base of operations on the Mincio passed through the country lying between Milan and Placentia, he hoped that, by adopting this plan, he would be able to assemble his forces in this space, seize the roads there, and thus completely sever the Austrian communications and place Melas in a position where he must fight under a great disadvantage. With the French in possession of these roads, Melas would be compelled to concentrate and fight in order to recover his communications and save his army. In doing so he would be forced to raise the siege of Genoa and to abandon the attempted invasion of France.

Fifth: Should Bonaparte succeed in concentrating his forces as here set forth, the advantages of his position would be immense. The St. Gothard and Simplon routes in his rear would give him a safe retreat into the great stronghold of Switzerland in case of defeat; the Ticino would protect his right flank, the Adda his left; and the fertile plains of the Po would furnish the necessary supplies for his men and animals, while he was making ready to fight the Austrians or awaiting their attack.

Such are the principal reasons that decided Bonaparte to march the Army of Reserve into that part of Italy lying between the Po and Switzerland. But, having decided on this course, he had yet to determine whether he would lead the Army of Reserve across the Great St. Bernard, or march it into Switzerland and thence descend into Italy by way of the St. Gothard or the Simplon. It will be remembered that for a time he was undecided as to what course to take, and did not fully make up his mind until some time after the Army of Reserve had assembled at Lake Geneva.

In several respects the safest course that Bonaparte could have taken was to conduct his army into Switzerland, unite it with Moncey's corps, and march on Milan by way of the St. Gothard Pass. Had he adopted this course, he would have entered Italy with united forces along a single line of operations, and would have avoided the dangerous flank march from Ivrea to Milan within the enemy's territory. At this time his objective was Milan. His purpose was to assemble his army and the corps of Moncey in that vicinity. By crossing the Great St. Bernard with the Army of Reserve, while Moncey marched by way of the St. Gothard Pass, Bonaparte gave Melas the opportunity of concentrating the Austrian forces between the Army of Reserve and Moncey's corps, and of crushing each in turn with superior numbers.

In the comments on Moreau's operations in Germany, it has already been remarked that it is always a dangerous operation to attempt a concentration upon some designated place within the enemy's lines, for, as a rule, the enemy can mass his forces there more rapidly than the commander of an invading army; that in fact many a campaign has failed because the commanding general has attempted to concentrate his scattered forces upon some point within the territory held by the enemy. By so doing he gives the enemy a chance to assemble his forces between the separated columns of the attacking army, and to bring superior numbers against each column in succession. Yet in these operations Bonaparte not only committed this error, not only did what he had condemned Moreau for doing, but he also violated the principle which he himself had so often set forth and had so often exemplified, namely, *not to invade a country with a double line of operations.*

Why then did Bonaparte take this course? To answer satisfactorily this question it is necessary to bear in mind that, at this time, Suchet was fighting greatly superior forces on the Var, and that Masséna was in desperate straits at Genoa. The problem before Bonaparte was not merely to assemble his forces in the vicinity of Milan, but so to assemble them there as to stop the projected invasion of France and bring speedy relief to Masséna.

The most direct route from Lake Geneva to Milan is by way of the Great St. Bernard Pass, and thence through northern Italy. Had, therefore, Bonaparte taken the longer route through Switzerland by way of the St. Gothard, the Austrians, in the meantime, could have forced the crossings of the Var, and have compelled Masséna to surrender. Indeed, these events were the more likely to happen, inasmuch as the Army of Reserve, during its march through Switzerland, would not threaten in the least the Austrian communications.

The importance of crossing the Great St. Bernard with the Army of Reserve is seen in the fact that no sooner had French troops appeared in the valley of the Aosta than Melas at once withdrew ten thousand men from Suchet's front and ordered them to march on Turin. Thus, by the mere crossing of the Great St. Bernard with the Army of Reserve, the projected invasion of France was brought to an end. It was inevitable that such should be the case; for as soon as the French appeared in the extreme northern part of Italy, their mere presence there threatened the communications of the Austrians. It was therefore necessary that Melas should abandon the invasion of France, in order to destroy, if possible, the French troops that were threatening his rear. In war, it will ever be thus. No commander can afford to take the risk of pushing forward to new conquests so long as his communications are seriously threatened by his enemy.

Again: it will be remembered that no sooner had Melas learned that the Army of Reserve was marching on Milan than he sent orders to General Elsnitz to abandon the Var and to General Ott to raise the siege of Genoa. Even the mere knowledge of Bonaparte's destination, before the movement on Milan had actually been completed, was of itself sufficient to cause Melas to change immediately his entire plan of campaign. Had not Masséna, at the time, been just on the point of giving up Genoa, General Ott would not have delayed there two or three days to await the capitulation. In fact, had Masséna known of the exact state of affairs, he doubtless would have held out a day or two longer, and saved himself the humiliation of a surrender. Even without a battle, the concentration of the French forces between Milan and Placentia would, in a short time, have set free Masséna's soldiers; for Melas would then have been obliged to concentrate and fight, in order to recover his communications and connect with his base of supplies. Bonaparte saw clearly this fact. Though he did not know how

long Masséna could hold out at Genoa, he realized
that matters there were rapidly approaching a
crisis, and that it was of the utmost importance
that the Army of Reserve should reach Milan at
the earliest possible moment. He realized that
upon the direction given his columns and upon
the rapidity of their movements depended the
fate of Suchet on the Var and of Masséna at
Genoa.

Other reasons, too, deterred Bonaparte from
marching the Army of Reserve through Switzerland. In this rough and mountainous country,
supplies could not be easily obtained. Especially
was this true of the St. Gothard route, which had
been overrun by the French during the two
previous years. Besides, this route was reserved
for Moncey's corps, which, of itself, would tax
to the utmost the resources of the country. Moreover, this road, a mere bridle path in places,
passes through narrow defiles and across lofty
and rugged mountains. Evidently a large army
issuing into Italy by this route would be so
stretched out that the advance divisions could
be defeated before the rear divisions could re-
enforce them.

The Simplon route was shorter than the St.
Gothard route, but the difficulties to be overcome
on each were of the same character. Inasmuch,
however, as Lake Maggiore lies between these
two routes, it will be observed that, had Bona-

parte advanced into Italy by way of the Simplon, while Moncey marched by way of the St. Gothard, Melas might have assembled a strong force at the foot of the lake, and, from his central position, have thrown superior numbers against each French column in succession. In this way he might have defeated both in detail before they could have united at Milan.

The principal reasons why Bonaparte chose the Great St. Bernard route having been considered, it will now be of interest to point out the several courses that he might have taken after having descended the Alps into the lower valley of the Aosta. It will be remembered that on the 27th of May Bonaparte was between Ivrea and Chivasso with thirty-five thousand men, and that Melas was at Turin with sixteen or seventeen thousand. At this time Bonaparte might have taken any one of three courses. He might have advanced on Turin, driven back Melas, united with Thurreau's division at Susa, and thus have secured his communications with France by the Mont Cenis route; or he might have crossed the Po at Chivasso, attacked and driven Melas from Turin, then have marched on Genoa by way of Alessandria; or, lastly, he might have marched on Milan, and there have united his army with Moncey's corps. In his memoirs Napoleon himself has discussed the advantages and disadvantages of these plans as follows: —

"Of these three courses, the first was contrary to the true principles of war. Since Melas had considerable forces with him, the French army, therefore, would run the risk of fighting without having a certain retreat, Fort Bard not being then taken. Besides, if Melas should abandon Turin and move on Alessandria, the campaign would be a failure, and each army would find itself in its natural position : the French army resting upon Mont Blanc and Dauphiné ; and that of Melas with its left at Genoa, and in its rear the fortified places of Mantua, Placentia, and Milan.

"The second course appeared impracticable : how hazardous would have been the situation of the French between the Po and Genoa, in the midst of an army so powerful as that of the Austrians, without any line of operations [1] (communication), any assured retreat.

"The third course, on the other hand, presented every advantage : the French army, once in possession of Milan, would secure all the magazines, depots, and hospitals, of the enemy's army ; it would join the left under General Moncey, and have a safe retreat by the Simplon and St. Gothard. The Simplon led to the Valais and Sion, whither all the magazines of provisions for the army had been sent. The St. Gothard led into Switzerland, of

[1] In his memoirs and in other places Napoleon often speaks of "lines of operations," meaning "lines of communication." Every advancing army must necessarily have a line of operations. If the roads leading from an army to its base are held by the enemy, the army is said to have lost its communications ; in other words, to have lost its line of communication with its base of operations. The point that Napoleon intended to make in the discussion is this : Fort Bard being at the time in possession of the Austrians, the French army had no unobstructed line of communication back to its base of operations at Lake Geneva ; hence, if defeated, it would find great difficulty in retreating by this route.

which we had been in possession for two years, and which was covered by the Army of the Rhine then on the Iller. In this position the French general was at liberty to act as he pleased ; if Melas should march with his whole army from Turin upon the Sesia and the Ticino, the French army could give him battle with this incalculable advantage, that, if it should be victorious, Melas, with his retreat cut off, would be pursued and driven into Savoy ; and if it should be defeated, it could retreat by the Simplon and the St. Gothard. If Melas, as it was natural to suppose, should move towards Alessandria in order to join the army coming from Genoa, it might be hoped that, by advancing towards him and crossing the Po, he might be met and be forced to fight before he could reach Alessandria. (In other words, before the troops of Melas, and of General Ott, coming from Genoa, could unite at Alessandria.) The French army having its rear secured by the river, and by Milan, the Simplon, and the St. Gothard ; while the Austrian army, having its retreat cut off, and having no communications with Mantua and Austria, would be liable to be thrown upon the mountains of the western coast of Genoa, or entirely destroyed, or taken at the foot of the Alps, at the Col di Tenda and in the county of Nice. Lastly, by adopting the third course, if it should suit the First Consul, when once master of Milan, to suffer Melas to pass, and to remain between the Po, the Adda, and the Ticino, he would thus, without a battle, reconquer Lombardy, and Piedmont, the Maritime Alps, and the Genoese territory, and raise the blockade of that city ; these were flattering results to anticipate."

Bonaparte has been severely criticised for not taking the second course, which he has so briefly

discussed in his memoirs. It has been repre-
sented that in marching on Milan, he sacrificed
Masséna, when he might have marched directly
to the relief of Genoa by way of Alessandria, and
thus have saved his lieutenant the humiliation of
a surrender. But what are the facts? They are
that Melas sent orders to General Ott to raise the
siege of Genoa before the Army of Reserve had
even reached Milan. Had, therefore, Bonaparte
crossed the Po at Chivasso, attacked and driven
back Melas, and marched on Alessandria, he
could not have brought relief to Masséna any
earlier.

If Bonaparte had crossed the Po, he could undoubtedly have defeated Melas and driven him
back to Alessandria; but here the Austrian commander, protected by the fortifications of the city,
would doubtless have made a stand, and would
have collected a large force to oppose Bonaparte.
In this position, Melas would be joined by General Elsnitz, already marching on Alessandria,
and could receive re-enforcements from General
Ott and from General Vukassovich. Thus, in a
short time, he could outnumber Bonaparte's army.
Moreover, at Alessandria he could prevent the
junction of Moncey's corps with the Army of
Reserve, and might possibly be able to defeat
them in detail.

In this position, Bonaparte, if defeated, would
have no unobstructed line of retreat, for Fort

Bard was still held by the Austrians; and, if victorious, he could do no more than force Melas back along the great highway to Mantua. In fact, should Melas be defeated at Alessandria, he could fall back to the fortress of Tortona or to the Stradella Pass, and there occupy another strong position. Here, with the re-enforcements that would doubtless join him from Genoa, from Vukassovich's corps, and from the fortresses in his rear, he would still have great chances of success.

In short, it would have been the height of folly for Bonaparte, with no secure line of retreat, to march into the centre of the Austrian theatre of operations, and expect to conquer Italy with but thirty-five thousand men. Even though it had been necessary to sacrifice Masséna, Bonaparte would have been justified in marching on Milan; for, in no other way could he be joined by Moncey's corps; in no other way could he sever the Austrian communications, and in no other way could he hope to defeat Melas and conquer Italy. Victory was his object.

The most critical part of Bonaparte's operations was the flank march from Ivrea to Milan; for at this time his only line of retreat was by way of the Great St. Bernard; and even on this route the Austrians still held Fort Bard.

Under ordinary circumstances, a flank march is always more or less a hazardous undertaking.

When a commander makes this movement and is attacked in route, he must form front to a flank,[1] and fight with his battle-line parallel to his communications, while the enemy can fight with his front perpendicular to his communications. In this position the advantage of the enemy is enormous. If victorious, he severs the communications of his adversary, and may then capture or destroy his army; if defeated, he can retreat in safety along his communications, or fall back to a new position, fight again, and thus prolong the conflict. An army without communications is like a rudderless ship adrift on the ocean. In order to fight, soldiers must have food and ammunition. No greater calamity, short of defeat, can befall a commander than to be cut from his base of operations and lose his source of supply.

Had, therefore, the Army of Reserve been defeated while marching from Ivrea to Milan, it would have lost its line of communication by way of the Great St. Bernard. In that case it would undoubtedly have been captured or destroyed; for since the Italian entrances of the St. Gothard and Simplon passes were then held by ten thousand Austrians under Vukassovich, Bonaparte could not have retreated into Switzerland.

That Bonaparte appreciated the critical features of the situation is seen in the skill with which he

---

[1] An army *forms front to a flank* when it operates on a front parallel to the line communicating with its base.

planned and executed the march. By ordering
Lannes to make preparations to cross the Po at
Chivasso, Bonaparte gave Melas the impression
that the French intended to cross the Po and
attack the Austrians near Turin. Thus Melas
was deceived. Meanwhile Bonaparte, with the
greater part of the Army of Reserve, marched
rapidly on Milan. During the march Lannes
descended the Po towards Pavia, thus covering as
with a screen the movements of Bonaparte. So
skilfully were these manœuvres made that Melas
did not even attempt to cross the river, in fact, did
not even learn of the march of Bonaparte until the
29th of May, two days after the movement had
begun. On the 31st Bonaparte arrived on the
Ticino; and on the 2d of June, having driven
back Vukassovich's corps, he entered Milan.
Here the critical part of his march ended, for he
was then sure of being joined by Moncey's corps,
and had, in case of need, a safe line of retreat
into Switzerland by the St. Gothard and Simplon
passes.

Another circumstance that aided Bonaparte in
this march was the presence of Thurreau's division
of four thousand men at Susa. Melas, being
ignorant of the strength of this division, hesitated
to push forward and attack Lannes, so long as
these troops remained undefeated on his flank and
rear. On this point General Hamley makes the
following comments: —

" Thurreau's force, being entirely separated from the main army throughout the operations, was useful only as leading the enemy to a false conclusion. But its value in that respect was incalculable. There were sufficient Austrian troops round Turin to check Thurreau and crush Lannes, thus laying bare the rear of the French army. But the road of the Mont Cenis was both more practicable and more direct than that of the St. Bernard ; moreover, Thurreau had artillery, and Lannes, at first, had not, for his guns had been delayed by the difficulties of passing the Austrian fort of Bard. It was but a natural error, therefore, for Melas to believe that Thurreau was backed by the whole French army."

Upon his arrival at Milan a threefold problem confronted Bonaparte. His object was to prevent the escape of the Austrians, to preserve his communications with Switzerland, and, in case of an Austrian attack, to make a quick concentration for battle. The skill with which he solved this complex problem will become apparent, if we turn to the map and study the positions of the French forces immediately after the arrival of Moncey's corps. These forces numbered fifty-five thousand men. Thirty-two thousand were stationed along the Po from Placentia to the Stradella Pass on the great highway leading from Alessandria to Mantua; ten thousand were stationed on the Ticino; ten thousand on the Adda; and three thousand at Milan. Thus it will be seen that these forces were occupying the sides of the triangular space enclosed by the Ticino, the

Po, and the Adda; and that they held possession of all the roads leading from the Alps to the Austrian base of operations on the Mincio. The ten thousand men on the Ticino not only protected the Italian entrance to the St. Gothard on the west side, but they were in a position to dispute the passage of the Ticino, should Melas cross to the north side of the Po and attempt to reach Mantua by way of Pavia and Milan. In the event that Melas should adopt this plan, the resistance that these ten thousand men could offer him would give Bonaparte time to unite all his forces for battle on the north side of the Po. The thirty-two thousand men on the south side of the Po closed with a barrier of steel the great highway leading from Alessandria to Mantua. On this road they had fortified a camp at the Stradella; and across the Po they had constructed five bridges, which would enable Bonaparte, in an emergency, to recross the river rapidly with these troops. The ten thousand men along the Adda not only covered the Italian entrance to the St. Gothard on the east side, but they were in a favorable position for holding in check Vukassovich's corps, should it attempt to march westward to the relief of Melas. It will be observed, too, that, should Melas attempt to escape by marching to Genoa, and thence to Mantua by way of Bobbio and Placentia, the French forces about Placentia and along the Adda could delay the progress of

the Austrians long enough for Bonaparte to concentrate all his forces against them.

Occupying a triangle in the heart of northern
Italy, the French corps and divisions supported
one another. In a few hours Bonaparte could
concentrate nearly the whole of his army on the
Po, on the Ticino, or on the Adda. In this position he held complete possession of the Austrian
communications, and had his own with Switzerland strongly guarded. In this position he could
concentrate quickly, and fight with nearly every
advantage in his favor.

"Napoleon has told us," says Colonel Hart,
"that the whole art of war — the secret of success
— consists in being strongest at the decisive
point." Even when making a great flank or turning movement against his enemy, Napoleon kept
this principle constantly in view. Thus, in these
operations, though at the outset the several
columns under his immediate command, numbering nearly sixty thousand men, entered Italy
from different directions, separated by interven-
ing obstacles and great distances, yet, by deceiv-
ing his adversary and by skilful manœuvres, he
succeeded in conducting fifty-five thousand men
into such positions that they could, in an emergency, support one another on a single battle-field.
His theory of war was concentration. His constant endeavor was to outnumber the enemy in
battle. In order to accomplish this result, he

nearly always made a great effort to call in his detachments just previous to a general engagement. His skill in strategy consisted in so directing his columns that when needed they could be quickly assembled on the battle-field. His skill in war consisted in the fact that he nearly always brought greater numbers against his enemy on the day of battle, even when he was outnumbered within the theatre of operations. On the battle-field, too, when it was impossible to outnumber his adversary, his quick eye discerned the vital point, the key of the position, so to speak; and there, neglecting the less important points, he massed his troops and overwhelmed his enemy. But in this campaign, strange to relate, after the battle of Montebello, and prior to the battle of Marengo, he seemed to neglect the principle of calling in his columns. When he assembled his forces south of the Po in the Stradella Pass, he felt certain that Melas would shortly advance eastward from Alessandria to attack him; yet he issued no orders for his forces north of the Po to join him. Again: at Marengo he was outnumbered, while ten thousand French soldiers along the Ticino, but a short distance away, had not a single Austrian in their front.

Inasmuch as Bonaparte held the crossings of the Po between Pavia and Cremona, he could easily have assembled the greater part of his army on the south side of the Po, and have brought greatly superior numbers against Melas. But Bonaparte feared that, if he adopted this plan, Melas might cross the Po and make his escape by way of Pavia and Milan. It will be remembered that, just prior to the battle of Marengo, Bonaparte was completely in the dark as to the movements of his adversary. He did not know but that the Austrian commander was making preparations to escape. As a matter of fact Bonaparte had lost touch of his enemy. He was in a state of confusion and uncertainty as to the intentions of Melas. He could not understand why the Austrians did not march eastward from Alessandria and attack the French, unless it was because they were about to attempt their escape by way of Pavia and Milan, or by way of Genoa. Had Bonaparte known the true state of affairs; had he known that the Austrians would soon cross the Bormida to attack the French, undoubtedly he would have assembled on the battle-field the ten thousand men stationed along the Ticino. That he did not do so was an error; perhaps, under the circumstances, an unavoidable one, but nevertheless an error, for he was outnumbered at Marengo when he might easily have outnumbered his adversary. In fact, nearly all his operations after the battle of Montebello are open to criticism. They are not up to the standard of the ordinary operations of Napoleon. His forces were scattered when they might have been united. He attempted too much. In order to win everything, he incurred unnecessary hazard. In order to prevent the Austrians from escaping, he took too great a risk on the battle-field.

It will be borne in mind that it is easy for any one, having a fair knowledge of the science of war, to point out, after the event, the mistakes that were made. During active operations confusion and doubt are constant factors that cannot be ignored by a commander. Neither Bonaparte nor his officers knew, or could know, the facts as we know them to-day. Thus the military student is able, after months of study, to point out the errors made by a great master of war. He approaches the subject from a different point of view from that of the commanding general. He is cognizant of facts, many of which at the time were unknown to the head of the army. He writes in the light; Napoleon marched in the darkness. He has the details of the campaign at his finger's end; Napoleon had to form his conclusions from the doubtful information at hand. Thus it is that mediocrity can criticise what genius alone can conceive and execute.

Again: it must be remembered that the really great soldier is not he who never makes a mistake, but he who in the aggregate makes the fewest mistakes. In war the conditions are such that a commander cannot by any possibility

always know the truth. He must often decide
momentous questions on the spur of the moment,
basing his decisions on unreliable information
obtained mostly from reports and rumors. "Speak
to me of a general who has made no mistakes in
war," says Turenne, "and you speak of one who
has seldom made war." "In the profession of
war," says Napoleon, "the game is always to the
one who makes the fewest mistakes."

If Bonaparte had withdrawn all his forces to the
south side of the Po, Melas might have made his
escape by way of Pavia and Milan, but even then
Bonaparte would have won northern Italy without
a battle. Had Melas taken this course, it is evident that he would have severed the communications of Bonaparte with Switzerland. Though
the loss of the French communications would
doubtless have inconvenienced Bonaparte, it would
not have put a stop to his active operations, nor
have proved fatal to his army; for he could then
have united his forces with those of Suchet, and
have at once established another line of communication with France by way of Nice. On this
point General Hamley, one of the greatest of
military critics, comments as follows: —

"There was a special circumstance in this campaign
which should have induced Napoleon to bring his whole
army to the south bank. For if Melas moved through
Milan he would leave the country south of the Po clear
for Napoleon to establish another and better communi-

cation with France by the south of the Apennines, and, moreover, a junction with Suchet would be effected, and the territory which was to be the prize of the campaign would be lost to the Austrians. But Napoleon could not be satisfied to let the enemy escape, even at such a sacrifice of territory, and therefore it was that he left the Ticino guarded."

In studying these operations, one cannot but be struck by the fact that Bonaparte seemed extremely anxious to retain his communications with Switzerland. The arrangement of his forces was admirable for this purpose. Even when he fought at Marengo, he had unobstructed communication across the Po to Milan, and thence to the St. Gothard Pass. Rather than weaken his communications by withdrawing his forces from the Ticino, he seemed to prefer the hazard of battle with a superior enemy. In a critical examination of these operations, it is almost impossible not to come to the conclusion that Bonaparte had a good reason for holding on to his communications with Switzerland. Being at the head of the French government, he had control of the armies of the Republic. He had crossed the Alps to conquer. Much depended on his success, for his own destiny hung in the balance. Undoubtedly he intended to return to France triumphant, whatever should be the cost. He was bold enough to stake all on a single throw — to hazard his own and his country's fate on a single battle.

If he should be defeated at Marengo and be driven out of the valley of the Po, might he not retreat through Switzerland into Germany with the remnants of his forces? Might he not unite them with Moreau's army, crush Kray in the valley of the Danube, march on the Austrian capital, and "conquer Italy at Vienna"? Is it not possible that this may have been the reason why he held on so persistently to his communications with Switzerland?

In this discussion it has just been assumed that Bonaparte might have been driven out of the valley of the Po. But this assumption is altogether improbable. Even if Bonaparte had been defeated at Marengo, the chances of his success on another field in Italy would still have been greatly in his favor. It needs but a glance at the situation to substantiate this statement. It is evident that if Melas had been victorious at Marengo, he would have attempted to open up his communications with Mantua, by marching eastward from Alessandria through the Stradella Pass. His victorious troops would have numbered at the most but twenty-three thousand men. Doubtless Bonaparte, while holding the Stradella Pass with the detachment already there, would have fallen back across the Po with the remnants of his defeated forces, numbering not less than eighteen thousand men; and would have united them with his columns on the north side of the

river.   In this way he could have collected in a
short time on the north bank of the Po an army
of about forty thousand men to oppose the twenty-
three thousand under Melas.   In this position the
French communications would have been in no
danger; but the Austrians, in order to recover
their communications, would have been obliged to
force the intrenched camp of the Stradella; which
operation would have given Bonaparte time to
cross the Po and attack the Austrians in flank.
Having the advantage of position and an overwhelming superiority in numbers, Bonaparte
would undoubtedly have crushed and destroyed
the army of Melas.   If this statement seems too
strong, reflect a moment, remember that during
his entire career Napoleon never lost a battle in
which he outnumbered his adversary.

In the result of the victory at Marengo is seen
the brilliancy of Bonaparte's strategy.   Having
finally won the battle, northern Italy as far as the
Mincio at once fell into his hands.   Notwithstanding the fact that he failed to outnumber his
enemy on the battle-field of Marengo, his strategy
was such that he could fight there with the assur-
ance that he would lose little if he were defeated,
but would gain much if he were victorious.

On the other hand, Melas fought the battle,
knowing that he must conquer or lose all.
Already his communications were in the hands
of Bonaparte.   Nothing short of overwhelming

victory could wrest them from the French. Though Melas did not know the number of French troops in his front, yet, having once decided upon the course to take, he made an heroic effort to save his army. Courageously he faced the inevitable. Brave man that he was, when the time came he fought as a soldier should fight.

After the battle of Montebello, Bonaparte united near the Stradella Pass all his forces south of the Po. Here he collected twenty-nine thousand men. Being deficient in cavalry and artillery, while Melas was well supplied with both, Bonaparte decided to occupy this strong position, where his flanks would be protected by the Po on one side and by the spurs of the Apennines on the other. He had every reason to believe that Melas would shortly advance from Alessandria, cross the Scrivia, and attempt to cut his way through the French army. If, therefore, Bonaparte should push westward from the Stradella, he must expect to meet the Austrians in the plain lying between the Scrivia and Bormida rivers. Here, however, the superiority of the Austrians in cavalry and artillery would give them a great tactical advantage. On the plain their artillery would have full sweep, and their cavalry could manœuvre with freedom against the flanks of the French. Moreover, Bonaparte believed that the Austrian forces, under the immediate command of Melas, outnumbered those of the French.

It was, therefore, neither wise nor prudent for Bonaparte to leave this strong position and march westward into the plain of Marengo. Other reasons, however, caused him to take this course.

First: He feared lest the Austrians should escape. While he remained in this position, they might march on Genoa, or cross the Po at Valenza, thence proceed to Pavia and force the crossings of the Ticino.

Second: He wished to attack and defeat the Austrians under Melas before they could be re-enforced by the numerous other Austrian detachments scattered throughout Italy. Bonaparte had already delayed his movements several days to await the arrival of Moncey's corps. During the delay Masséna had surrendered. Now, Bonaparte was anxious to bring matters to an issue before other advantages should accrue to the Austrians.

Third: Though from a tactical point of view the chances of success in the open country were unfavorable to Bonaparte, yet from a strategical point of view they were greatly in his favor. He had severed the Austrian communications by closing the great highway leading from Alessandria to Mantua. Along the Ticino he had a strong force to prevent Melas from escaping in that direction; in the Stradella Pass he had established a fortified camp; and from Pavia to Cremona he held the line of the Po, across which he had constructed five bridges that could be used for a retreat in case he should be defeated. In the open country, therefore, a defeat would, at the most, be but a temporary check, for he could fall back, cross the Po, unite his defeated troops with the French forces on the north side of the river, and be ready in a short time to fight another battle. On the other hand, since the communications of the Austrians were already in possession of the French, the defeat of Melas must result in the capture or destruction of his army, and in the loss of northern Italy. It follows, therefore, that in the plain of Marengo Bonaparte could gain much more by a victory than he could lose by a defeat.

Fourth: He never was satisfied to take up a defensive position, and there await an adversary. He seldom fought defensive battles. He believed in the offensive. His method of making war was to march and to fight. It was necessary to seek the enemy, to meet him face to face, to crush him on the battle-field.

At the battle of Marengo, Bonaparte was surprised. Having but a small cavalry force under his immediate command, he held it in reserve in rear of his infantry in order that it might, in case of battle, be used against the Austrian cavalry, which greatly outnumbered his own. Had he ordered it to the front to seek the Austrians and to screen the movements of Victor and Lannes, doubtless he would not have remained completely in the dark as to the position and intention of his enemy. It has been said that "Cavalry are the eyes of an army." Certainly for the want of it at Marengo, or for the failure to use what he had for screening and reconnoitring purposes, Bonaparte lost touch of his enemy.

Again: when he found that the village of Marengo was not occupied in force by the Austrians, he was led to believe that Melas was trying to escape. He was still further confirmed in this belief by the result of the reconnoissance made on the 13th of June from Marengo towards Alessandria. Though the Austrians were occupying the bridge-head on the right bank of the Bormida and the two bridges in rear of it, the French officer in command of the reconnoitring party failed to learn this fact. Indeed, he reported that no Austrians were to be found in force along the Bormida. Dumas tells us that "Bonaparte would not go to bed until he made sure whether the Austrians had a bridge over the Bormida. At one o'clock in the morning the officer in charge of this mission returned and reported that it did not exist. This announcement quieted the First Consul. He required a last account of the position of his troops, and went to sleep not believing that there would be an engagement the next day." This false information deceived Bonaparte. It was, in fact, one of the causes that led to his defeat on the following morning.

If this reconnoitring party had done its duty, Bonaparte would undoubtedly have been prepared for battle. In that case he would have held on to Desaix, and would have concentrated his forces at Marengo and along the Fontanone. Had he occupied this position with twenty-eight thousand men, he might have defeated the Austrians in detail as they crossed the Bormida. Even had Melas succeeded in crossing the Bormida with his entire army, he would then have been obliged to fight a great battle with an unfordable river directly in his rear. Thus situated, the defeat of Melas must have resulted in the capture or annihilation of his army.

For several days Melas hesitated whether he should cross the Bormida and attack the French. Owing, however, to the fact that he did not decide until the 13th of June to attack Bonaparte, he neglected to occupy Marengo. This neglect permitted Victor to occupy the village, and aided him materially in resisting the attacks of the Austrians on the next day. Yet, on the whole, this blunder of Melas proved to be more advantageous to the Austrians than to the French; for it led Bonaparte to believe that Melas had no intention of crossing the Bormida and of attacking the French in the plain of Marengo.

In sending two thousand five hundred cavalry to Acqui to watch Suchet, Melas committed an error that probably lost him the battle. There was little or no excuse for this error; for Suchet was so far away that he could not possibly arrive at Marengo in time to take part in the battle. Had Melas kept this cavalry force on the battle-field, and thrown it vigorously against the French as they fell back towards San Giuliano, he would undoubtedly have won the battle. It was the failure of the Austrians to pursue the French promptly that enabled Bonaparte to rally the scattered remnants of his defeated forces near San Giuliano. Says Colonel Hart:—

"When a great battle is imminent, it is unwise for a commander to detach any part of the force available, unless he is very confident of victory. There are many examples in history of misfortune, or misfortune narrowly escaped, in consequence of doing so. Melas would, in all probability, have made perfectly certain of the victory at Marengo, if he had not unnecessarily detached 2500 cavalry to arrest the march of Suchet, who was at too great a distance to be taken into consideration. Napoleon himself at Marengo, although ultimately victorious, was as nearly as possible defeated because he detached Desaix to reconnoitre towards Rivalta; indeed, he was at first defeated, but the return of Desaix restored the battle."

It is here worthy of notice that while Melas was sending away this detachment of two thousand five hundred men, Bonaparte was making every effort to hasten the return of the six thousand men under Desaix.

At the sound of the first cannon-shot at Marengo,

Desaix faced about his command and hurried forward to aid Bonaparte. It was fortunate that the First Consul had Desaix for a lieutenant at Marengo. Had Grouchy marched to the sound of the cannon at Waterloo, and supported his chief as loyally as did Desaix at Marengo, Napoleon might never have fallen.

If Suchet, who was at Acqui with the remnants of the Army of Italy, numbering about twenty thousand men; had pushed on vigorously towards Marengo, and had arrived there on the morning of the 14th of June, the battle would have been decided in favor of the French early in the day. Such a movement would have given Bonaparte an overwhelming superiority in numbers, and would probably have resulted in the destruction or capture of the whole army of Melas.

That Suchet did not take this course was due to several causes. The soldiers of the Army of Italy had just finished a great fight. They had already performed heroically their part in the great struggle. Many of them, too, having starved and suffered at Genoa, had become so emaciated that they could hardly bear the weight of their equipments. Moreover, Suchet, who was still acting under the orders of Masséna, had been cautioned not to peril his army by advancing too far. Inasmuch as Bonaparte had been more than twenty days in Italy, and had not yet destroyed Melas, Masséna was somewhat doubtful of the outcome.

Consequently he wished to hold the Army of Italy well in hand, so that, in case Bonaparte should be defeated, it could fall back to the Var, and, being there re-enforced from the departments of southern France, make another effort to save France from invasion.

On the morning of the 14th of June the forces of Melas concentrated at Alessandria numbered thirty-two thousand men. He held the two bridges spanning the Bormida, and the bridge-head on the right bank. On the opposite side of the river the French forces available for battle numbered twenty-two thousand men. In addition, Desaix's division, if it could be recalled in time, would increase the French forces to twenty-eight thousand. Early in the day Melas had despatched two thousand five hundred men of his reserve cavalry on Acqui. It will thus be seen that the opposing forces at Marengo were about equal in strength: the Austrians numbered twenty-nine thousand five hundred men; the French, twenty-eight thousand. But at the outset the advantages were greatly in favor of Melas. He outnumbered Bonaparte in both cavalry and artillery, and the plain of Marengo was especially favorable to these arms. His forces were united; the French were scattered. Desaix's division was marching on Novi; and the remainder of Bonaparte's forces extended over a distance of ten miles from Marengo to and even beyond the

Scrivia. Moreover, Bonaparte was not expecting
a battle. Thus it happened that when the Austrians crossed the Bormida, the French were surprised and outnumbered. At first Victor bore
the brunt of the fight; then he and Lannes were
attacked by nearly the whole Austrian army. By
the time Bonaparte arrived on the field with the
Consular Guard, the reserve cavalry, and Monnier's division, Victor was crushed and Lannes
badly shattered. It was then too late for the
re-enforcement under Bonaparte to turn the tide
of battle. That too was soon overwhelmed. In
short, Melas defeated the French forces in detail.
During that morning he was always stronger
than his adversary at the decisive points.

In the afternoon all was changed. The Austrians were scattered; they stretched from
Marengo to San Giuliano. Moreover, they were
marching carelessly and had no expectation that
Bonaparte would attack them. Meanwhile,
Desaix had returned, and Bonaparte's forces had
rallied behind the hillocks near San Giuliano.
In a short time Bonaparte overthrew the advance
under Zach, then proceeding westward, gathering
momentum and strength as a result of his first
success, he outnumbered and crushed in succession the several Austrian organizations. Thus
the Austrians were defeated in detail in the afternoon as the French had been defeated in the
morning. Here again is seen the necessity of

outnumbering an enemy at the vital point of the battle-field. Courage and heroism on the field of battle are of little avail, unless a commander concentrates his forces and outnumbers his adversary at the decisive point. The brain of the commanding general is the birthplace of victory.

In this battle the genius of Bonaparte is seen, not in the knowledge he displayed of his adversary's doings, for Bonaparte was completely surprised at Marengo; not in the arrangement of his forces, for that could hardly have been worse; not in any deeds of surpassing courage, for no one could excel the heroism of Lannes on that battle-field; but in his complete mastery of the situation, — in the fact that, amidst turmoil, ruin, and death, he saw just when and where and how the blow should be struck to change disaster into victory. This was the merit of Bonaparte at Marengo. On that field he was a great tactical captain. While the storm of battle was at its height, and the dying and the dead were around him, he was cool, clear-headed, and vigilant. While disaster was staring him in the face, he saw the vulnerable spot in the formation of his adversary's forces, and by massing troops there, crushed and overwhelmed them.

In this campaign Bonaparte was fortunate in having a Masséna at Genoa, a Suchet on the Var, and a Lannes at Montebello and at Marengo. He was fortunate, too, in having a Desaix near at hand, who dared march to the sound of the cannon, and who counselled hope when he might have counselled despair.

Though these operations of Bonaparte were brilliant in strategic manœuvres and in far-reaching results, nevertheless they were faulty in execution. Out of a total force of fifty-five thousand men, the greater part of whom might have been present on the battle-field of Marengo, only twenty-eight thousand fought there. Instead of calling in his detachments before the engagement, and of outnumbering his enemy on the battle-field, as had always been his plan heretofore, he permitted himself to be outnumbered by Melas. Rather than let a single Austrian escape, he took great chances on the battle-field. In short, he attempted to grasp too much; and, by doing so, sacrificed a certain amount of safety. Doubtless within his breast there was the feeling that he would stake all and abide by the consequences. Reckless of the sequel, he pressed on with the faith of a fatalist, little realizing how much glory and how much gloom yet remained in store for him. It would seem that his triumph was written in the stars; perhaps, too, his fall was written there.

CHAPTER V.

GENERAL COMMENTS.

WHILE the Army of Reserve was assembling near Lake Geneva, only a few people at Paris knew that Bonaparte himself intended to take command of it. In fact, a provision in the constitution of the Year VIII. did not permit a consul to command an army in person. But, as Bonaparte himself said, it did not prevent his being present with the army; moreover, this constitutional provision was then regarded by the French people, and even by the Senate and Tribunate of France, as having no binding effect on Bonaparte. Nevertheless, the First Consul did not wish to violate it openly, and, accordingly, adopted the subterfuge of making General Berthier the nominal commander in chief, retaining in his own hands the entire conduct of the campaign. To all intents and purposes, therefore, Bonaparte was the real commander of the Army of Reserve.

Having assembled the Army of Reserve at Lake Geneva, he was in a position where, if the necessity should arise, he could march to the assistance either of Moreau in Germany or of

Suchet on the Var. Had Melas succeeded in forcing the Var, Bonaparte would doubtless have marched south along the west side of the French Alps in order to unite the Army of Reserve with Suchet's forces for an attack against Melas. The strategical skill of Bonaparte appears in this arrangement. Though he expected to cross the Alps, yet up to the last moment his army was so situated that he was prepared for any contingency that might arise.

Though the campaign of Marengo, as planned and executed by him, was a bold and hazardous undertaking, yet a careful analysis of the operations shows that nearly all of them were marked by extreme caution. It will be found, too, that his strategy was almost perfect for accomplishing his ends. In fact one of the great merits of Napoleon was that he knew how to produce a maximum effect with a minimum force. The whole theatre of war was an open book to him. He saw just where the battle should be fought in order to produce the greatest results. Though the Austrians in this campaign numbered nearly a quarter-million of men, and stretched from the Gulf of Genoa to the Main River, yet Bonaparte was able, while still at Paris, to picture in his mind the whole strategical situation, and to indicate Stokach in Germany and the Stradella Pass in Italy, as being the two most important points within this immense theatre of operations. These two places were the keys of the territory occupied by the two Austrian armies. Here the greatest results could be produced with the smallest efforts. Here, in each case, a victory could be obtained with the least loss to the French.

Bonaparte's caution is seen in the fact that he would not set out to cross the Alps until Moncey's corps was well on its way towards Italy. Before beginning the movement, he wished to be certain that he would receive this re-enforcement, and to make sure of his communications with Switzerland. He knew that he might be attacked in the plains of Piedmont before he could reach Milan, and might lose his communications by way of the Great St. Bernard Pass. If, however, Moncey succeeded in reaching Italy, Bonaparte would then have uninterrupted communications with the great stronghold of Switzerland.

Again: his caution is seen in the fact that, after descending the Alps with the Army of Reserve, he immediately took measures to concentrate his forces, instead of crossing the Po at Chivasso and of marching directly to the relief of Masséna. He knew that a great battle was inevitable, yet safety was his first object. He wished to gain a position where he could bring a strong force on to the battle-field, and where, if defeated, he could retreat without losing his army. In fact, throughout the campaign, he kept a watchful eye upon his communications. It was his rear that gave him the greatest anxiety. It is always so with the great masters of war. "While the distant spectator," says Hamley, "imagines a general to be intent only on striking or parrying a blow, he probably directs a hundred glances, a hundred anxious thoughts, to the communications in his rear, for one that he bestows on his adversary's front." Notwithstanding the fact that Napoleon seemed always to take great chances in his military career, and seemed often to stake everything on the fate of a single battle, yet a careful analysis of his campaigns shows that no commander has ever looked with more anxiety to his lines of retreat than did this great master of war. At Austerlitz, where he allowed the enemy to envelop his right and cut off his retreat on Vienna, and where he was so certain of success that he issued a proclamation in advance explaining the manœuvre by which victory would be obtained, yet even here he had provided for a retreat through Bohemia in case of defeat.

This campaign was indeed a bold one; but it must be remembered that the very boldness of Bonaparte was one of the principal causes of his success. By descending the Alps into Italy upon the Austrian rear, he surprised his adversary and caused him to tremble for his communications. By this means he struck terror into the heart of Melas even before a battle had been fought. No sooner had French troops reached the valley of

the Po than Melas was compelled to change his
whole plan of campaign. He had then to defend
himself against Bonaparte. He could no longer
think of invading France. By this bold movement Bonaparte snatched the initiative from his
adversary and compelled him to fight on the
defensive. In war, the boldest course is often
the safest. "The greatest soldiers have always
been the most daring."

From the discussion in the preceding chapter,
it is evident that in this campaign Bonaparte
allowed his boldness to outrun his caution. He
attempted to grasp too much. This characteristic
of Napoleon, here exhibited for the first time in
his military operations, was in after years one of
the principal causes of his fall. In his subsequent career he fought Spain and Portugal on one
side and nearly the whole of Europe on the other.
Though the greatest exemplar of concentration
that the world has ever known, yet at times he
divided his forces when he should have made
peace on one side, and have concentrated on the
other. In the Russian campaign, too, he was
overconfident. He was not satisfied with ordinary
victories or with ordinary results. His early
successes were so marvellous that he began to feel
that he could conquer in the face of all Europe,
and in spite of the elements themselves. And
yet this very boldness, coupled with a caution
that seldom failed him, was one of the secrets

of his numerous victories during so many years of war.

The crossing of the Alps with the Army of Reserve was undoubtedly a hazardous undertaking, yet it was so carefully planned in all its details that it was completely successful. During the operations of Masséna in Italy, and of Moreau in Germany, Bonaparte had displayed marvellous energy in hastening the preparations for crossing the great chain of the Alps. In this famous passage, nothing, however trivial, that could contribute to the success of the operation was beneath the attention of Bonaparte. Referring to the activity and care displayed by the First Consul at this time, Thiers, in his "History of the Consulate and Empire," writes as follows:—

"Himself toiling day and night, corresponding with Berthier, who was organizing the divisions of infantry and cavalry; with Gassendi and Marmont, who were organizing the artillery; with Marescot, who was reconnoitring the whole line of the Alps; he urged every one to exertion, with that headlong energy and ardour which sufficed him to carry the French from the banks of the Po to the banks of the Jordan, from the banks of the Jordan to those of the Danube and Borysthenes. He would not leave Paris in person until the last moment, not wishing to abandon the political government of France, and leave the field clear to intriguers and conspirators for a longer time than was absolutely necessary. Meanwhile, the divisions ordered from La Vendée, from Brittany, from Paris, and from the banks of the

Rhone, traversed the widespread territory of the Republic, and the heads of their columns were already appearing in Switzerland. The depots of some corps were still at Dijon, besides some conscripts and volunteers, sent thither to give credence in Europe to the opinion that the army of Dijon was a pure fable, destined solely to alarm Melas. Up to this moment everything had gone well; the illusion of the Austrians was complete. The movement of the troops advancing towards Switzerland was little noticed, because the corps were so much dispersed, that they passed for re-enforcements sent to the army in Germany. . . . To such a point had he carried his foresight as to establish saddlers' workshops at the foot of the defile, for the repair of the artillery harness. On this apparently trivial matter he had already written several letters; and I mention this circumstance for the instruction of those generals and governments to whom the lives of men are intrusted, and who too often, through indolence or vanity, neglect such particulars. Nothing, in fact, that can contribute to the success of operations, or to the safety of soldiers, is below the genius or rank of commanding officers."

One of the secrets of Napoleon's success in war was the fact that he bestowed great care on all military matters. Whether his operations were simple or complex; whether his attention was called to the ration of a single soldier, or to the subsistence of a hundred thousand men; whether his mind was occupied with the trivial details of routine duty, or was evolving the grandest strategic conceptions, he was the same painstaking, orderly, careful man. "His plan," says Napier, referring to Napoleon's projects in the war with Spain, "embraced every probable chance of war, and even provided for the uncertain contingency of an English army landing upon his flanks at either end of the Pyrenean frontier. Neither his power nor his fortune nor the contempt he felt for the military power of the Spaniards made him remiss. The conqueror of Europe was as fearful of making false movements before an army of peasants as if Frederick the Great had been in his front."

In the campaign of Marengo Bonaparte displayed excellent judgment in selecting his subordinates. However much he may have failed in this respect in his subsequent career, certainly at this time his success was due in great measure to the fact that he selected Masséna to command the Army of Italy, and Moreau to command the Army of the Rhine.

Masséna was peculiarly fitted both by birth and character to perform the duty required of him. Born at Turbia near Nice, he was familiar with every foot of country bordering on the Gulf of Genoa. Moreover, he had fought in the same theatre of operations under Bonaparte in 1796–97. In action he was cool, clear-headed, obstinate, and brave. When the battle was at its height, and the struggle fierce and desperate, then his genius shone forth with great brilliancy. Probably no other soldier of France could have made such an heroic struggle at Genoa. Though he had some traits of character that stained his reputation and dimmed his glory, he was nevertheless a great soldier, perhaps the greatest of all those remarkable men who were afterwards made marshals of France. His characteristics were thus set forth by Napoleon at St. Helena: —

"Masséna was a man of superior talent. He generally, however, made bad dispositions previous to a battle, and it was not until the dead fell around him that he began to act with that judgment which he ought to have displayed before. In the midst of the dying and the dead, of balls sweeping away those who encircled him, then Masséna was himself — gave his orders and made his dispositions with the greatest *sang froid* and judgment. . . . By a strange peculiarity of temperament, he possessed the desired equilibrium only in the heat of battle; it came to him in the midst of danger. The sound of the guns cleared his ideas and gave him understanding, penetration, and cheerfulness. He was endowed with extraordinary courage and firmness. When defeated he was always ready to fight again as though he had been the conqueror."

Though Moreau failed to appreciate thoroughly the strategical situation in Germany, nevertheless the First Consul showed wisdom in appointing him to command the Army of the Rhine. Moreau was familiar with this theatre of operations, and possessed the confidence of the soldiers under him. Moreover, he was brave and cautious, and wonderfully cool and collected on the battle-field. Though he failed to do all that he might have done, yet he was generally successful, and, on the whole, justified the confidence bestowed on him by the First Consul.

In this connection it is worthy of remark that Desaix was ranked by Napoleon as one of the greatest of his subordinates. Had he not been killed at Marengo, he would undoubtedly have been made one of Napoleon's marshals. At St. Helena Napoleon spoke of him as follows: —

" Of all the generals I ever had under me, Desaix and Kléber possessed the greatest talents — especially Desaix ; as Kléber only loved glory inasmuch as it was the means of procuring him riches and pleasures, whereas Desaix loved glory for itself, and despised everything else. Desaix was wholly wrapped up in war and glory. To him riches and pleasure were valueless, nor did he give them a moment's thought. He was a little, black-looking man, about an inch shorter than I am, always badly dressed, sometimes even ragged, and despising comfort or convenience. When in Egypt, I made him a present of a complete field-equipage several times, but he always lost it. Wrapt in a cloak, Desaix threw himself under a gun, and slept as contentedly as if he were in a palace. For him luxury had no charms. Upright and honest in all his proceedings, he was called by the Arabs *the just Sultan.* He was intended by nature for a great general. Kléber and Desaix were a loss irreparable to France.".

It is worthy of remark that many of the generals that fought in the French armies during these operations afterwards became marshals of Napoleon. In the Army of Italy there were Masséna, Soult, and Suchet; in the army of Reserve, Lannes, Victor, Murat, Berthier, Marmont, and Davoust; and in the Army of the Rhine, St. Cyr, Moncey, and the immortal Ney, "the bravest of the brave."

The knowledge that Bonaparte displayed of his adversaries' doings in this campaign is indeed wonderful. From reports sent him by Suchet, Masséna, and Moreau, and from information obtained from spies, he had not only a knowledge of the positions occupied by the Austrian armies, but, in addition, was accurately informed as to their numbers and plans of operations. A single example will suffice to illustrate the accuracy of his information, and his remarkable intuition, before the beginning of hostilities, as to the movements and plans of Melas. It will be remembered that while still at Paris he wrote to Masséna as follows: —

"The enemy will debouch upon your right in the direction of Genoa, on your centre in the direction of Savona, and probably on the two points at once. Refuse one of the two attacks, and throw yourself with all your forces united, upon one of the enemy's columns. . . . In that broken country, if you manœuvre well, with 30,000 men you may give battle to 60,000 ; in order to carry 60,000 light-armed troops into Liguria, Melas must have 90,000, which supposes a total army of 120,000 men at least."

Compare now the prediction of Bonaparte with what happened. Melas *had* one hundred and twenty thousand men. He advanced against Masséna in two columns: one, numbering twenty-five thousand men, divided into two parts, advanced on Genoa; the other, forty thousand strong, advanced on Savona. The movements of Melas were carried out exactly as Bonaparte had predicted. In the letter to Masséna, the Austrian plan, as well as the numbers with which Melas was about to attack the Army of Italy, were set forth with wonderful accuracy. When it is remembered that at this time Bonaparte was at Paris, and that the great chain of the Alps intervened between him and the Austrians in Italy, no one can fail to be impressed by the foresight of Bonaparte and the accuracy of this prediction made before the event. Wellington once said that he had been trying all his life to find out what the other fellow was doing over the hill. Bonaparte, at Paris, knew what Melas was doing over the hill.

In the campaign of 1796–97 in Italy, Bonaparte had shown himself a consummate master of tactics and of strategy. In the campaign of Marengo he exhibited, in addition to these qualities, great organizing power. When he returned from Egypt, civil war existed in certain parts of France, the finances were in a deplorable state, and the French armies had been everywhere defeated.

In a few months, under his leadership, all was changed. He crushed out the civil war, placed the finances on a firm basis, sent re-enforcements to the Army of the Rhine, and organized the Army of Reserve. Referring to this period, Alison says:—

"The sudden resurrection of France, when Napoleon assumed the helm, is one of the most extraordinary passages of European history. . . . After the fall of the Committee of Public Safety, the triumph of France centered in Napoleon alone; wherever he did not command in person, the greatest reverses were experienced. In 1795 the Republicans were defeated by Clairfait on the Rhine; in 1796 by the Archduke Charles in Germany. In 1799 their reverses were unexampled both in Italy and Germany; from the 9th Thermidor to the 18th Brumaire, a period of about five years, the fortunes of the Republic were singly sustained by the sword of Napoleon and the lustre of his Italian campaigns. When he seized the helm in November, 1799, he found the armies defeated and ruined; the frontier invaded both on the sides of Italy and Germany; the arsenals empty; the soldiers in despair, deserting their colours; the Royalists revolting against their government; general anarchy in the inteterior; the treasury empty; the energies of the Republic apparently exhausted. Instantly, as if by enchantment, everything was changed; order reappeared out of chaos, talent emerged from obscurity, vigour arose out of the elements of weakness. The arsenals were filled, the veterans crowded to their eagles, the conscripts joyfully repaired to the frontier, La Vendée was pacified, the exchequer began to overflow. In little more than six months after Napoleon's accession, the Austrians were forced to seek refuge under the cannon of Ulm, Italy was regained, unanimity and enthusiasm prevailed among the people, and the revived energy of the nation was finally launched into a career of conquest."

At the beginning of the campaign of Marengo, Kray's army, numbering one hundred and twenty thousand men, occupied western Germany. The army of Melas, one hundred and twenty thousand strong, occupied northwestern Italy; a British corps of twelve thousand was in Minorca, and a British fleet in the Gulf of Genoa.

To oppose the forces of the allies, Bonaparte had three armies: the Army of the Rhine, numbering one hundred and thirty thousand men, was facing the Austrians in Germany; the Army of Italy, forty thousand strong, was along the Apennines and Maritime Alps; and the Army of Reserve, numbering forty thousand, was assembling near Lake Geneva. It will thus be seen that the allies had two hundred and fifty-two thousand men to oppose the two hundred and ten thousand under the First Consul; and that they possessed the additional advantage of being supreme on the sea.

Such was the situation in the spring of 1800. On the 5th of April Melas began active operations along the Apennines. On the 14th of June the campaign ended at Marengo. In two months and ten days the French, guided by the genius of Bonaparte, had compelled Kray to seek safety in the fortified camp of Ulm, and had defeated Melas and gained possession of northern Italy. These great results were due to Bonaparte. It was he that crossed the Alps. In his brain was born the strategy that led to victory.

In this campaign Bonaparte calculated carefully every movement; he left nothing to chance. Though fortune favored him in many ways, nevertheless his success was due to his genius and to his mastery of his profession. Strategically these operations were almost perfect, yet they were faulty in execution. "The campaign of Marengo," says William O'Connor Morris, "at least in design, was one of the most dazzling of Napoleon's exploits in war. The plan of issuing from Switzerland by a double movement in the rear of the enemy in Swabia and Italy was perhaps equal to any formed by Hannibal; but the execution of it was far from perfect. Moreau completely failed to cut off Kray. Napoleon made a distinct mistake in marching into the plain of Marengo, and he exhibited in this instance a fierce resolve to encounter his adversary at any risk, which cost him dear on more than one occasion. The most striking feature of this part of his career is the restoration of order in France, her sudden and rapid rise out of misfortune, and the revival of her military power; and though this was largely due to the energy and resource of a great nation not often quelled by disaster, it should perhaps be mainly ascribed to Napoleon's genius." At this time Bonaparte was thirty years of age; he was vigorous in mind and body. He was ambitious, and had a massive determination to succeed. He had a will which no obstacle could daunt, a mind original, bold, profound, quick, and penetrating. His eye pierced the depths and reached the heights of things. With a marvellous intuition he was able at times to foresee just what course his adversaries would take. So accurate was his information, so profound his knowledge of military matters, that he was often able to predict what, under certain conditions, would happen. "He had," says Morris, "a faculty of organisation perhaps never equalled, and a power of calculation, a force of insight and industry, and a capacity of mastering details, which Nature has seldom bestowed on man." Moreover, he had made a profound study of the campaigns of the great commanders, and had read many books of history, the perusal of which, says Lamartine, "changes theories into actions, and ideas into men." In short, he was a consummate master of war. The fact that he was a great organizer, a great tactician, and a great strategist, is the real reason why he was so successful in war. Among all other great soldiers of the world, it would be difficult to select a single one who possessed in so marked a degree all these qualities. As an organizer, he was not excelled by either Cæsar or Alexander; as a tactician he was equal to Marlborough or Frederick; as a strategist, he surpassed every soldier of ancient or of modern times. Take him all in all he was, perhaps, the foremost soldier of the world.

Twenty-one years after this campaign, the Emperor Napoleon lay dying at St. Helena. His thoughts were with his army. During a long delirium, while a fierce storm was raging on the island, he was heard to say: "mon fils . . . l'armée. . . Desaix." These were his last words. Perhaps, amidst the shock of the billows and the battle-like roar of the storm, the great captain believed himself once more with Desaix on the tumultuous field of Marengo.

INDEX.

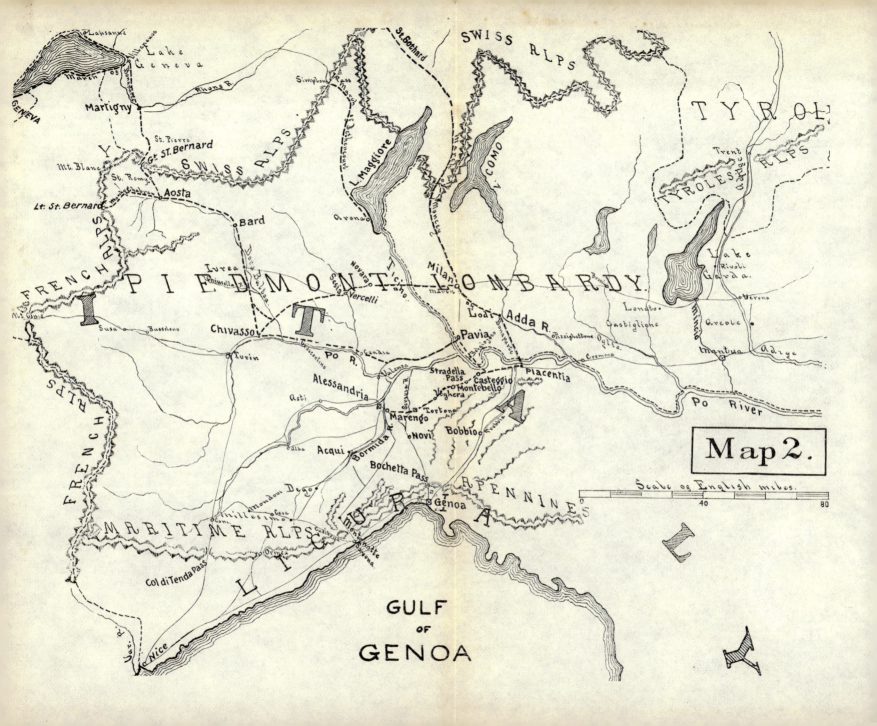

Map 2.

Scale of English miles.
0   40   80

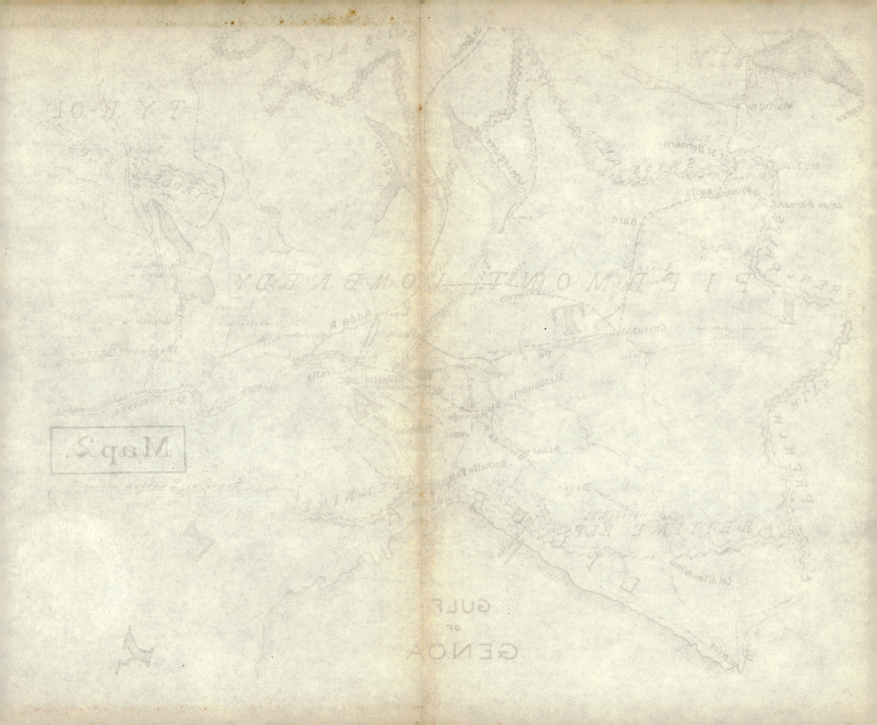

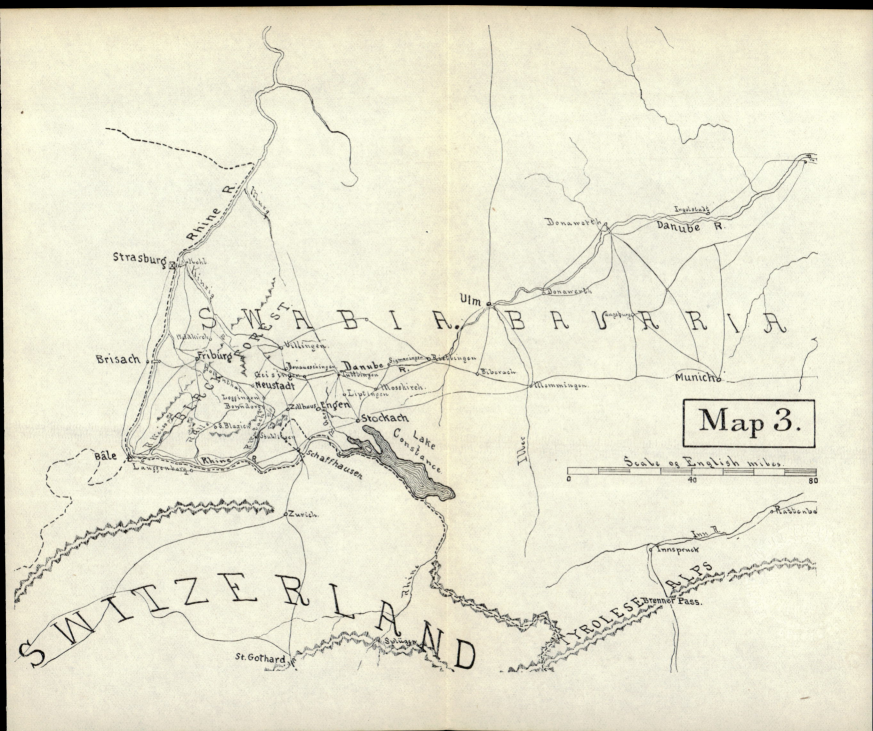

Map 3.

Scale og English miles.
0   40   80

Rhine R.

Strasburg Nehl

Brisach

Friburg

Neustadt

BLACK FOREST

SWABIA

Villingen

Donaueschingen Danube R.

Kreisingen

Liptingen Mosskirch

Loggingen Boyndorg

S.S.Blazien

Stuhlingen

Engen

Zollhaus

Stockach

Sigmaringen Riethlingen

Biberach

Memmingen

Lake Constance

Schaffhausen

Laugenburg

Rhine R.

Bâle

Zurich

SWITZERLAND

St.Gothard Splugen

Ulm

Donaworth

Donaworth

Ingolstadt

Danube R.

BAVARIA

Augsburg

Municho

Iller

Inn R.

Rattenbe

Innspruck

TYROLESE Brenner Pass.

ALPS

Rhine

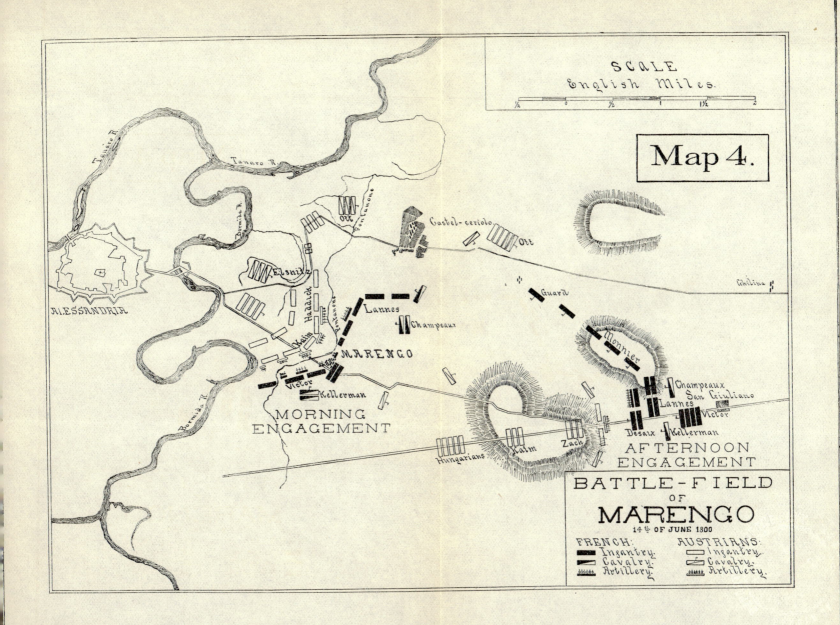

SCALE
English Miles.

Map 4.

Tanaro R.

Tanaro R.

Bormida R.

Fontanone

Castel-ceriolo

Ott

Ott

Chilina

Elsnitz

Haddich

Pirkenent

Kaim

ALESSANDRIA

Lannes

Champeaux

Guard

Monnier

MARENGO

Victor

Kellerman

MORNING
ENGAGEMENT

Champeaux
San Giuliano

Lannes

Victor

Desaix

Kellerman

Hungarians

Kalm

Zach

AFTERNOON
ENGAGEMENT

BATTLE-FIELD
OF
MARENGO
14th OF JUNE 1800

FRENCH: AUSTRIANS:
Infantry.   Infantry.
Cavalry.   Cavalry.
Artillery.   Artillery.

NAPOLEON BONAPARTE'S FIRST CAMPAIGN.

With Comments by HERBERT H. SARGENT, First Lieutenant Second Cavalry, United States Army.   Crown 8vo.   231 pages, with maps. $1.50.

SINCE its publication this work has received the enthusiastic praise of Press and Public, and has taken an important, and in many respects a unique, place in the ranks of Napoleonic contributions.

The peculiar conciseness and lucidity of the style, and the discriminating avoidance of technical and unessential details, have invited the attention of a non-military public ; while the preservation of the strategic essence of the history has insured for the work a permanent interest to the student of the art of war.   The book has been officially recognized by the United States Government, — the War Department having purchased one hundred copies for distribution in the service ; and it has received the hearty commendation of the commander in chief of the British army.

SOME COMMENTS FROM THE AMERICAN PRESS.

The Nation, New York.

The work is so clearly done, and the sketch maps so well illustrate the successive stages of the campaign, that the general reader can follow the story with satisfaction, and understand wherein Bonaparte was really great.

The Outlook, New York.

So carefully and accurately written is this volume, that the *London Times* pays our compatriot the compliment of begging him to continue his history through the other campaigns of Napoleon.

New York Herald.

Our author has been unusually successful in presenting his subject in such a plain and easily comprehended fashion, that if we know nothing about the strategy of the battlefield we follow him with increasing curiosity and pleasure.

Chicago Evening Post.

The author's method of study is simple : to give a careful yet simple description of a battle and then to comment upon it.   Its non-technical character and the fascination of its subject make it an acceptable volume for popular reading.

(OVER)

LAUREL-CROWNED LETTERS

LAUREL-CROWNED VERSE.

Edited by FRANCIS F. BROWNE.

THE LADY OF THE LAKE. By SIR WALTER SCOTT.

CHILDE HAROLD'S PILGRIMAGE. A Romaunt. By
LORD BYRON.

LALLA ROOKH. An Oriental Romance. By THOMAS
MOORE.

IDYLLS OF THE KING. By ALFRED, LORD TENNYSON.

PARADISE LOST. By JOHN MILTON.

THE ILIAD OF HOMER. Translated by ALEXANDER POPE.
2 vols.

Each volume is finely printed and bound; 16mo, cloth, gilt tops,
price per volume, $1.00.

In half calf or half morocco, per volume, $2.50.

*All the volumes of this series are from a specially prepared
and corrected text, based upon a careful collation of all the more
authentic editions.*

———

The special merit of these editions, aside from the graceful form
of the books, lies in the editor's reserve. Whenever the author
has provided a preface or notes, this apparatus is given, and thus
some interesting matter is revived, but the editor himself refrains
from loading the books with his own writing. — *The Atlantic
Monthly.*

A series noted for their integral worth and typographical
beauties. — *Public Ledger, Philadelphia.*

The typography is quite faultless. — *Critic, New York.*

For this series the publishers are entitled to the gratitude of
lovers of classical English. — *School Journal, New York.*

———

Sold by all booksellers, or mailed, on receipt of price, by

A. C. McCLURG & CO., PUBLISHERS.
CHICAGO.

LAUREL-CROWNED TALES.

ABDALLAH; OR, THE FOUR-LEAVED SHAMROCK. By ED-
OUARD LABOULAYE. Translated by MARY L. BOOTH.

RASSELAS, PRINCE OF ABYSSINIA. By SAMUEL JOHNSON.

RAPHAEL; OR, PAGES OF THE BOOK OF LIFE AT TWENTY
From the French of ALPHONSE DE LAMARTINE.

THE VICAR OF WAKEFIELD. By OLIVER GOLDSMITH

THE EPICUREAN. By THOMAS MOORE.

PICCIOLA. By X. B. SAINTINE.

AN ICELAND FISHERMAN. By PIERRE LOTI.

PAUL AND VIRGINIA. By BERNARDIN DE ST. PIERRE.

Handsomely printed from new plates, on fine laid paper, 16mo,
cloth, with gilt tops, price per volume, $1.00.

In half calf or half morocco, per volume, $2.50.

In planning this series, the publishers have aimed at a form
which should combine an unpretentious elegance suited to the fastidious book-lover with an inexpensiveness that must appeal to the
most moderate buyer.

It is the intent to admit to the series only such tales as have
for years or for generations commended themselves not only to
the fastidious and the critical, but also to the great multitude of
the refined reading public, — tales, in short, which combine purity
and classical beauty of style with perennial popularity.

A contribution to current literature of quite unique value and
interest. They are furnished with a tasteful outfit, with just
the amount of matter one likes to find in books of this class, and
are in all ways very attractive. — *Standard, Chicago.*

Sold by all booksellers, or mailed, on receipt of price, by

A. C. McCLURG & CO., PUBLISHERS,
CHICAGO

MASTERPIECES OF FOREIGN AUTHORS.

DOCTOR ANTONIO. By GIOVANNI D. RUFFINI.

THE MORALS AND MANNERS OF THE SEVENTEENTh CENTURY. Being the Characters of LA BRUYÈRE. Translated by HELEN STOTT. Portrait.

GOETHE'S WILHELM MEISTER'S APPRENTICESHIP AND TRAVELS. Translated by THOMAS CARLYLE. With Critical Introduction by EDWARD DOWDEN, LL.D. Edited, with notes, by C. K. SHORTER. Portrait. 2 vols.

PORTRAITS OF MEN. By C. A. SAINTE-BEUVE. Translated by FORSYTH EDEVEAIN. With Critical Memoir by WILLIAM SHARP. Portrait.

PORTRAITS OF WOMEN. By C. A. SAINTE-BEUVE. Translated by HELEN STOTT. Portrait.

NOVALIS (FRIEDRICH VON HARDENBERG). His Life, Thoughts, and Works. Edited and Translated by M. J. HOPE.

THE COMEDIES OF CARLO GOLDONI. Edited, with Introduction, by HELEN ZIMMERN.

In uniform 16mo size, cloth binding, per volume, 75 cents; half vellum, gilt top, per volume, $1.00.

This series comprises translations of single masterpieces by some of the best-known European writers, some of which have never before been presented in an English dress. The volumes are well printed on good paper, and very prettily bound.

The "Masterpieces of Foreign Authors" unite intr'nsic value with external attractiveness. — *Public Ledger, Philadelphia.*

The work of the translators is beautifully done, and the publishers have made dainty little volumes sure to win the appreciative regard of every book-loving eye. — *Chicago Times.*

Sold by all booksellers, or mailed, on receipt of price, by

A. C. McCLURG & CO., PUBLISHERS,
CHICAGO.

THE ELIZABETHAN LIBRARY.

A CABINET OF GEMS. Cut and Polished by SIR PHILIP SIDNEY; now, for the more Radiance, presented without their Setting by GEORGE MACDONALD. With portrait.

CHOICE PASSAGES from the Writings of SIR WALTER RALEIGH: Being a small Sheaf of Gleanings from a Golden Harvest. By ALEXANDER B. GROSART. With portrait.

A BOWER OF DELIGHTS: Being Interwoven Verse and Prose from the Works of NICHOLAS BRETON. The Weaver: ALEXANDER B. GROSART. With an Introduction on his Life and the Characteristics of his Writings.

"THOUGHTS THAT BREATHE AND WORDS THAT BURN," from the Writings of FRANCIS BACON. Selected by ALEXANDER B. GROSART.

GREEN PASTURES. Being choice Extracts from the Works of ROBERT GREENE, A.M., of both Universities, 1560 (?) 1592. Made by ALEXANDER B. GROSART.

"THE POET OF POETS." The Love-Verse from the Minor Poems of EDMUND SPENSER. ALEXANDER B. GROSART, Editor. With portrait.

"BRAVE TRANSLUNARY THINGS." From the Works in Prose and Verse of BEN JONSON. Selected by ALEXANDER B. GROSART.

THE FRIEND OF SIR PHILIP SIDNEY. Being Selections from the Works of FULKE GREVILLE LORD BROOKE. Edited, with an Introduction, by ALEXANDER B. GROSART.

24mo, gilt top, per volume, 75 cents.

A series of handy and tastefully printed little volumes, designed to bring the writings of some of the noble but little known authors of the sixteenth century before readers of the present day. The volumes are all printed in old-face type, on antique paper, in the 24mo size so characteristic of the sixteenth century, and are appropriately bound in the style of the Tudor period.

Sold by all booksellers, or mailed, on receipt of price, by

A. C. McCLURG & CO., PUBLISHERS,
CHICAGO.